ECCENTRIC
Kansas

ECCENTRIC
Kansas

TALES FROM ATCHISON
——— TO WINFIELD

ROGER L. RINGER
Foreword by Rebecca J. Tanner

THE
History
PRESS

Published by The History Press
Charleston, SC
www.historypress.com

First published 2019

Manufactured in the United States

ISBN 9781467144230

Library of Congress Control Number: 2019948154

I dedicate this book to the memory of my friend Carl Koster Jr.

A longtime friend, brother, boss and mentor.

Gone away too soon.

CONTENTS

FOREWORD

"The Three Pals"

There were three lifelong pals that at one time had lived together. They later were separated, and one lived in New York, one lived in California, and the other one was a Western Kansas farmer. They decided that it would be nice to leave this world together since they hadn't seen one another for some time. After arranging for the use of a large furnace, they placed themselves in it to be cremated. Three days later the New Yorker was taken out, and he was burnt to a crisp. The Californian was taken out next, and he was cooked very well done. The Western Kansas farmer was the last one to be removed. While he was being taken out, he remarked, "Another three days of this good hot weather, the wheat will be ready to cut."

–from William E. Koch,
"Tales, Tall and Short," *The Kansas Arts Reader*

———◆———

Kansans are known for their stories. Sometimes wild tales that pull our legs and tickle the funny bones. Telling those stories is a rite of passage. It gives us a sense of legacy and belonging. And it should be on the bucket list of every Kansan to repeat and retell the stories of past generations—for they are good stories and worthy of hearing again and again.

William Koch, who for decades taught Kansas folklore at Kansas State University, would tell the above story each semester to students. He would emphasize how every region of the state—every county—has stories to share. And although we identify as Kansans, some of our stories may be a little bit larger than life. Could we see a Western Kansas farmer comparing the summer's heat to a fiery furnace and noting its positive aspects for a wheat harvest? You bet. That's Kansas. We are quirky. We have our own brand of humor.

Roger Ringer, the author of this book, has dedicated it to one of his best friends, Carl Koster, a retired NFL photographer, former mayor of Cheney and promoter of rural Kansas. Koster, who died in 2018, spent his lifetime nurturing and capturing the legacy of Kansas scenes and stories.

Koster and his parents farmed southeast of Cheney. His grandfather had worked for the Jewett Stock Farm, a five-thousand-acre ranch near Cheney, and was able to acquire land east of the ranch shortly after the turn of the twentieth century. Mr. Koster's father was a musician who played in local bands during the Great Depression years and war years. Growing up during the 1950s, Koster was a 4-H'er and developed his photography skills doing 4-H projects. As an adult, he selflessly gave his time volunteering at county and state fairs as a photography judge.

Koster, like Ringer, appreciated the history of Kansas. He loved a good story. He would have loved the stories in this book.

During the nearly seventeen decades that Kansas has been a state, we Kansans have been innovative, creative, penny pinchers, academic, prudish, big spenders, adventuresome, farmers, artists, explorers, teachers and students. In short, we have been just about everything.

What we haven't always been is good promoters of our own state. We are known often for being humble—and a bit shy. But we are solid characters, and like that Western Kansas farmer in William Koch's folk tale of three friends, we endure. We continually prepare for the next harvest, the next big thing.

And like Carl Koster, we look to share our skills and talents.

—BECCY TANNER
Kansas journalist, teacher and historian

INTRODUCTION

*A*fter the publication of *Kansas Oddities*, the number one question to me during book signings was, "Are you going to write another one?" The manuscript I first submitted had more than 120,000 words in it, which left me with enough stories for nearly two more books already done. And I have been accumulating even more story ideas.

Yes, I would like to turn this into a series or a set. I guess we will see how things go on this one. The original passion that started this whole mess has not slowed down any. This whole thing boils down to one thing: I LOVE KANSAS!

There is also the question, "What would you generalize as a typical Kansan?" After the many stories that I have found and researched, I still cannot answer this question. In a government survey (which I am still amazed to see from a government that has to borrow money to give away), Kansas ranked fifth in the most people leaving and moving elsewhere. What do these people find so attractive about leaving a state that has so much and so much opportunity? I am dismayed.

I place part of the blame for that trend on the lack of education of Kansas history. The state requirement for the study of what the state has been is directly affecting what Kansas will become. It seems to be a popular thing to not be satisfied with where you are. Americans have always looked over the next hill, but the frontier days are long over. "The grass is always greener on the other side of the fence" is as true now as when the idiom was coined.

INTRODUCTION

What I love about Kansans are the dreams and ideas that they are coming up with all the time. From the very beginning, those farm boys spent hour after hour thinking, "There has to be a better way to do this." To say they had their heads in the clouds would not be very far off base. Kansans have been figuring how to fly for years, and the name "Air Capital of the World" is not something that was just thought up. We earned it!

Many Kansas communities have a favorite son or daughter who had ideas and gave the effort that it took to pursue their dream. But not every dream was successful. There are so many stories of the Kansans who had the idea and worked hard turning it into something. Some were successful, and many were not.

Through all the years that I have attended events on improving our communities and the state, I have had people who come up to me and tell me these stories, often starting with, "I bet you never heard this story about my town!" And most times I hadn't. I had a choice when I was not able to get around to all the areas of Kansas like I used to. I could sit around and brood about my failing health or I could start putting these stories down and preserve them before they are lost forever. Well, you can see the results. In fact, I am looking for ways to share my stories beyond these books. But that is another story.

I hope that you will enjoy this book as much as I have enjoyed finding the stories and presenting them to you here.

ECCENTRIC KANSAS

40 & 8

Near Garden Plain, there is a private lake with a chateau that is known locally but may not be familiar to many other people. It is called 40 & 8 Lake. Appreciating what this means takes us back to World War I. Troops coming to fight in the "War to End All Wars" were moved around the country of France in small boxcars. They were cramped and uncomfortable. The designation "40 & 8" means that the boxcar had a capacity of forty men or eight horses. A brief history that the 40 & 8 provides says that "the ability to laugh when the going gets rough is an important American trait."

The boxcars were called *voitures* in French. Marked "Hommes 40 / Chevaux 8," the trip in these *voitures* had to be handled with humor. It was said that the ride was so miserable that the men had to laugh. The rides in the *voitures* were only a taste of the misery that the troops endured in the war.

In Philadelphia in 1920, the idea of the 40 & 8 was created as a place for the veterans to get away to their own playground to blow off steam harmlessly and laugh at their troubles. The idea was so appealing to many in the American Legion that it quickly spread from Pennsylvania to the rest of the nation. But what started out as fun took a turn to more serious concerns.

In almost every town, the veterans could see that there were little children who were not having fun for themselves—unfortunate children who had lost fathers because of the war, whose dads were disabled or who were for other reasons unable to have happy childhoods. It was 40 & 8 money that started the American Legion's National Child Welfare Program. Money was earmarked for emergency aid for needy children in orphanages, hospitals and underprivileged areas.

Each member has an annual assessment from his dues to fund emergency needs of children regardless of race, creed or color. In the 1930s, the 40 & 8 spearheaded the campaign against diphtheria. After returning from World War II, Korea, Vietnam and other conflicts, many veterans needed hospital care, and there was a shortage of nurses. The 40 & 8 began sponsoring nurse programs and have had sponsorship programs for nurse training for years.

Another area that the 40 & 8 supports is Hanson's disease (leprosy). Members' efforts led to the elimination of outbreaks of the disease in medical facilities, and it has been declared practically incommutable.

La Société des Quarante Hommes et Huit Chevaux, also known as the "Forty & Eight," is a fraternal honor society of the American Legion. Each state has possession of one of the boxcars, or *voitures*, as a symbol of the organization. The Kansas *voiture* is in Lyons. Each post is known as a voiture

40 & 8 lake and chateau, Garden Plain, Kansas. *Courtesy of Larry Lampe.*

and is affiliated with the local American Legion post. The programs it supports include child welfare, nurse training, Americanism and the *Carville Star* (a national publication of the National Hanson's Disease Center).

Its stated purpose is as follows: "The Voyageurs Militaire of the Forty et Eight ask for nothing except to serve their fellow human beings and by that service to provide our children with a safe free land of opportunity, and to further provide for the adequate defense of the greatest system of government devised by the mind of man."

Just as the Garden Plain 40 & 8 facility has worked with the community on many projects, there are others as well. They go about their work quietly but always keep the welfare of the children and community in mind.

CHARLEY MELVIN: IOLA'S MAD BOMBER

Charley Melvin was born in Chicago and was raised in Bates County, Missouri, across the state line from Linn County, Kansas. He knew that he had a mission at an early age and believed he had been given visions by God to strike a blow against the power of rum. He made this statement to his wife, Etta, in a letter. For many years, he nurtured the vision and grew confident in what God had selected him for. "I am one of the few. I have been led by the spirit of God in the pillar of fire, just as truly as Moses was led by God." His family were extremely poor, with one daughter dying of starvation from being fed a diet of green beans and another daughter dying at birth.

Charley worked at Kansas Portland Cement Company and experienced bouts of sleeplessness. This had dragged on so long that he was afraid he would end up in "the madhouse." He went on a spree of buying firearms and then, for the purpose of "studying and learning" about the rum problem, purchased three bottles of beer and one bottle of whiskey and went on a drunken spree. It was probably because of a hellacious hangover that he decided to kill every "jointist" in town or die in the attempt. He was arrested before he could take action against the saloon keepers and was put in the state hospital at Osawatomie on January 4, 1905. He was forty-two at the time and had had a long list of stays at insane asylums. He remained there for four months and was released after being declared "cured."

On West Street in Iola, there was the Eagle, Blue Front and the Red Light Saloons, and these would be the targets of Charley's wrath. Standing in front of the Shannon Hardware store just over a block away from the saloons was Charley. The night was suddenly torn by a roar and a flash from an explosion at the Eagle from 150 sticks of dynamite. About one minute later, another massive explosion came from the Red Light, where Charley used 250 sticks of dynamite. He had never heard such an explosion. Without knowing how much damage had been done, he believed that it was a good deal more than he intended. He turned and disappeared into the night.

The explosion was heard as far as Humboldt, eight miles to the south; LaHarpe, six miles east; and Neosho Falls, ten miles to the northwest. One resident at Neosho Falls thought that the safe at the bank had been blown. Great holes were torn in the solid brick walls of the Red Light and the Eagle, and their roofs had caved in. James Thorpe was trapped in his second-floor bedroom. The buildings were destroyed, and many walls in buildings in the vicinity were damaged. Plate glass and windows were knocked out for blocks around. The new Allen County Courthouse took a tremendous blow, and its two-day-old clock was stopped by the explosion. Damages were estimated to total about $100,000 to the buildings (about $2.4 million in 2017 dollars).

After the bombing, the police searched for more dynamite. They found a sack with 112 sticks of dynamite with a partially burned fuse lying against the back wall of the Mills joint on the north side of Iola Square. Another bomb with 120 sticks of dynamite was found under the Campbell Saloon in Bassett, south of Iola.

Charley Melvin was not apprehended until August, while he was working in a railway camp near Keystone, Iowa. He was tried for burglary and theft of the dynamite. He pleaded not guilty by reason of insanity. The jury rejected the defense and sentenced him to fifteen years in the state penitentiary.

Due to his health, he was released from prison in June 1914. He died just a few months later from what was called tuberculosis of the intestines. He was not sent back to be buried in Iola because of the poverty of the family and the thought that the community would not appreciate him being buried there.

How does a community remember a mad bomber from so long ago? You have a festival, of course! Each year in July, the community has a Charlie Melvin Mad Bomber Race, including a 10K and a 5K. In the afternoon, there is a carnival, old-fashioned games and the Mad Bombing Drag Race (with prominent members of the community racing in drag). At midnight, the 10K is run, and twenty-six minutes later, the 5K begins. It is a run-walk.

EDGAR HENRY SUMMERFIELD BAILEY

"ROCK CHALK JAYHAWK K-U." Edgar Henry Summerfield Bailey is known for the creation of the most famous college chant, except that the original was "RAH RAH JAYHAWK K-U." With use, it morphed into the chant we hear today. But if this was Edgar's most famous act, it was by far not the most important.

Edgar was born in Middlefield, Connecticut, on September 17, 1848. After finishing district school, he attended Wesleyan Academy in Wilbraham, Massachusetts, where he became very interested in chemistry, physics and geology. From there he went to Sheffield Scientific School at Yale University, earning his bachelor's degree. He spent a year at Yale doing graduate work and teaching before taking his first full-time position teaching at Lehigh University, where he remained for seven years. In 1881, he attended Kaiser Wilhelm University in Strasbourg, Germany, under Dr. Rudolph Fittig. In 1895, he went to Leipzig, Germany, for further study. Many leading American scientists of the era went to Germany to study and do research.

Edgar received his Doctor of Philosophy degree from Illinois Wesleyan University in 1883. In the fall of 1883, he was appointed head of the University of Kansas Chemistry Department, being the only teacher in a time when the streets of Lawrence were still dirt and the town had boardwalks and common drinking cups. Disease was widespread, impure food was common and drinking water was polluted. Edgar's job for the next fifty years was to teach and do research. He was an expert in commercial chemical analysis, which allowed him to teach mineralogy, metallurgy and assaying.

At the time there was wide-scale water pollution, food impurities and practices that promoted the spread of disease. The Kansas Board of Health was formed in 1885, and pure food laws were passed in 1889, 1901 and 1905. At the same time, things were heating up on the national level with the publishing of the book *The Jungle*, on the abuses of the meatpacking industry. In 1906, Congress passed the Pure Food and Drug Act, which was signed into law by President Theodore Roosevelt. The Meat Inspection Act was passed in 1907.

Edgar, alongside other Kansans and specifically Dr. Crumbine of Dodge City, worked to change practices, introduced the concept of disposable drinking cups and prohibited the use of roller towels to reduce the spread of infection. One of the two state laboratories was established at KU, with the other being at the Kansas State Agricultural College (K-State). The

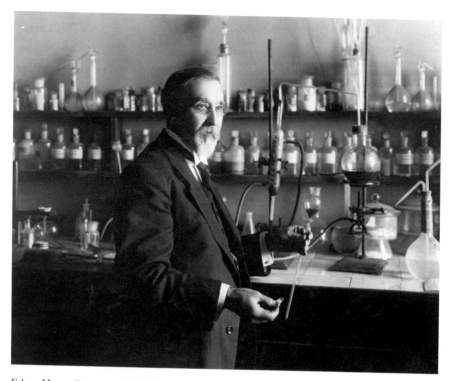

Edgar Henry Summerfield Bailey, originator of the University of Kansas chant which became "ROCK CHALK JAYHAWK K-U." *Courtesy of University of Kansas Library Archives, Kenneth Spencer Research Library.*

laboratory was in the KU Chemistry Department. With little funding, Dr. Crumbine personally purchased food items to be analyzed in the labs. The results of the lab analysis of the food products had a severe impact on the companies that followed poor practices. Many of the companies tried to work against the health staff, even resorting to offering bribes to change results. Later, actual funding and enforcement powers were given to the new Kansas Health Department.

Edgar's test results on a wide range of food adulteration had a major impact on the health of Kansas residents and practices throughout the industry. In order for the public to be aware of the practices of the adulteration of foods and food additives, he started to publish pamphlets to allow cooks to be able to test and identify foods and additives that were not safe for consumption. Also, the size of the containers was called into question, resulting in the passage of the Weights and Measures Act, which was placed under the control of the Kansas Board of Health. Also, the use of dyes and colorings for food was brought into question, as were other practices used to enhance the appearance of food items that had resulted in the increase of profits and the lessening of nutrition. Being the Kansas Board of Health's chemist meant that Edgar worked on research and conditions in the prisons and reformatories, state hospitals and industrial schools. Being concerned about the state's water resulted in the creation of the Kansas Geological Survey by the Kansas Regents. Under this body, Edgar conducted the first survey of the state's waters. With two other scientists, he coauthored the first Kansas Geological Survey. This work consisted of nine published volumes.

In the beginning, Edgar not only taught all the science classes at KU but also was responsible for the laboratory analysis for the state, as well as research into state resources. EHS Bailey's tenure at KU lasted from 1883 to to 1933. He had a major impact on the development of the state's industrial resources and always worked to protect the public.

BEECHCRAFT PLAINSMAN AUTOMOBILE

The aircraft industry had the foresight to see that the end of World War II was coming and that this would effectively end the huge contracts that the military had provided to anyone able to build something. The resumption of the civil aircraft industry would be uncertain, and being able to make it through an expansion of products to build and market would mean a company's survival. It would also save jobs for a workforce that was skilled and productive.

The engineering research department of the Beechcraft Aircraft Company had been working on two prototype Dodge hybrid gas/electric reconnaissance trucks. Based on the Dodge military recon wagon, both used Franklin flat air-cooled aircraft engines to drive a DC generator, motors and control systems. A General Electric assembly was used in one prototype and a Westinghouse in another. Each wheel would be driven independently by an electric motor. This gave equal traction to each no matter the road surface.

The units negotiated a forty-five-degree slope without difficulty. Braking was done by reversing the electrical polarity with a backup hydraulic system. Realizing that the program would outlive the war, the order was given to utilize the technology to build a civilian automobile. Thus, the development of the Plainsman automobile began. Development started after V-J Day in 1945 and resulted in the 1946 model Plainsman.

The unique-looking prototype resembled the Tucker and was just as advanced. Using aircraft technology, distinctive aircraft designs and techniques were evident. The standard-looking grill did not give away the engine unit, which could have been in the front or in the back. The resultant prototype had the engine and generator in a soundproof rear compartment. The rear styling was a bit boxy looking, but the tests in the wind tunnel proved the overall design to be very efficient and aerodynamic.

The passenger compartment featured a tall profile that promoted great visibility. There were auxiliary panes above the windows all around that afforded great headroom. The windshield was divided but curved outboard. The doors were cut into the roof, making entrance and exit easier, plus any protrusions were eliminated inside and out by using solenoid latches to open the doors. The chair high seats had a lot of head, shoulder and leg room for six adults.

The driver's bench had four-way electric adjustments, and the right passenger seat was a double lounge chair. Instruments and controls were grouped around the steering wheel. There was an "Econometer" planned to track fuel efficiency. The speedometer was in direct driver view above the steering column in a small black hooded pod. There were no seat belts, but there were leather covered pads on the dash and tops of the seats. Standard equipment included a two-way radio telephone.

Beechcraft Plainsman Car, one of two prototypes built. *From the* Hemmings Motor News.

The roof was structurally strong, even with the slim A pillars that gave great visibility. The rear design was boxy and limited driver visibility. Using electric motors on each wheel eliminated the differential, shaft, clutch, transmission and the drive shaft hump. This gave the Plainsman great room for six and reduced the weight. The frame and body parts were all aluminum. Acceleration was claimed to be better than conventional types of automobile designs. Top speed was 160 miles per hour, and it would make 25 miles per gallon at 60 miles per hour and 30 miles per gallon in town.

The price was set at $4,000 to $5,000. This would have put the price into the range of the Rolls-Royce category, but the expected market would be for the high-end driver. The car was never put into production because in 1947 the government gave Beechcraft $22.5 million in orders for aircraft. Whether it could have been built and been commercially successful is only conjecture. Even today, the technology would be applicable.

No one knows what happened to the prototype of the Plainsman or the Dodge Recon vehicles.

CLOUGHLEY MOTOR VEHICLE COMPANY

Robert H. Cloughley was living in St. Paul, Kansas, when he read an account of Cornelius Vanderbilt, who had imported a horseless carriage from France when he had visited there. It was a great sensation, and in a time when horses were the main mode of transportation, the idea of a horseless carriage was just not a concept of anything practical. Robert had a friend, H.A. Clark, who was also taken by the idea of a self-propelled carriage. Pictures of the Vanderbilt vehicle were published in papers and magazines all over the country.

Robert and Mr. Clark sent for every publication that had pictures and information on the horseless carriage. They studied the concept and started to experiment. Taking a farm wagon in 1898, they began to build a concept vehicle. Since Robert was an experienced railroader, he started with a steam engine and put together the first model. There was a lot of trial and error, and the working parts had to be designed, built and rebuilt to make things work properly.

Years later, Robert's son in Colorado reminisced about driving this automobile at age twelve around the streets of St. Paul. As they made the working model functional, they decided to bring the auto to Parsons, where they gave a demonstration. It was a hit, and the townspeople were excited about the new contraption driving up and down the streets. The Cloughley steam auto was so far ahead of its time that the horn had not been invented yet, so it was equipped with a bell. Horses were frightened even though it made less noise than a gasoline-powered auto.

The 1898 model demonstrated many design theories and proved to be a workable design. Work then began on a model that was more in the style of an automobile than a converted wagon. Many sources mention that the first production of the Cloughley steam motor vehicle was in Cherryvale. The Cherryvale Commercial Club did make overtures to build a factory there, but the factory ended up in Parsons. Robert and Clark ran up against many obstacles in the process of forming their company and building a factory. The year 1902 saw the first regular production of the Cloughley motor vehicle, but the $10,000 in capital that they started out with proved to be inadequate to really get things off the ground. The automobile that they built had the distinction of being the first commercially built automobile west of the Mississippi River—and one of the major reasons the company could not last.

The first reason that the Cloughley auto could not be successful was that it was too far ahead of its time. The acceptance of automobiles was not there yet. Not enough people were willing to give up their horses as their transportation, even when the reliability and durability of the auto had been proven. Distance travel was by railroad, and the concept of decent roads between towns was still years away. The second reason was the fact that it was the first automobile manufactured west of the Mississippi. The population numbers, supply companies, machine shops and basic materials were not close, so the autos were more expensive to build in Parsons. It is why Detroit and other manufacturing centers were successful.

By 1903, the company was out of business. Robert spent many years using one of his autos as a taxi in Parsons. Even though when they decided that the steam engine was not practical and built some models with gasoline engines, it was not enough. For the rest of his life, Robert was a house painter in the Parsons area. One article reported that Robert was working in Chicago and broke his arm when a motor that he was cranking backfired.

Robert passed away at age eighty on May 29, 1950, in Jackson County, Missouri. He was married to Mary Jane Duncan of Parsons. The couple had five children as of the 1900 census. In an interview with his son in Colorado Springs, he said that the first factory endeavor was in Cherryvale and the second in Parsons. He told the reporter that a dust-covered Cloughley

The Cloughley automobile, built in both gas and steam power. *Courtesy of the Parsons Historical Museum.*

was found in a barn and taken to the Henry Ford Museum. However, the museum cannot find any model of the Cloughley in its collection. It was supposed to be brought in, but there is no record of what happened to it. It is unknown if any of the one hundred produced have survived.

GODDARD'S BUSH PILOT

In the book *Arctic Bush Pilot* by pilot James Anderson, his definition of the "Greatest Alaskan Bush Pilot" was simple: "anyone who survived." And one of the names that comes up in the annals of bush pilots in Alaska is Goddard, Kansas native John Milton Cross. It has to make you wonder how that Goddard boy made it up to Alaska and made such a name for himself. Harmon Helmerick's book *The Last of the Bush Pilots* called John Cross the "master of close calls."

Cross was a survivor, and it all started as a pilot in Kansas. Logging more than twenty-two thousand hours in his flying career, he joined the U.S. Army Signal Corps in World War I. Afterward, he became a test pilot, barnstormer and airline pilot. Cross had the distinction of surviving a midair collision with Jimmy Doolittle in the early 1930s at Kansas City.

A graduate of the University of Kansas, Cross became a test pilot for Swallow Aircraft in Wichita. He also worked for Straughn Aircraft Company. He rebuilt surplus World War I airplanes while he barnstormed around the Midwest.

Jimmy Doolittle was flying for Shell Oil Company in a Travel Air Mystery S Racer. He had a spectacular way of making an approach and landing. He would dive several thousand feet, make a low-level pass across the airport, pull into a vertical climb and do two snap rolls straight up before winging over into his final approach.

Cross was making a final approach in a PT 3, not knowing that Doolittle was landing at the same time. Cross saw the racer at one thousand feet, but the racer hit the PT 3 from below and took the tail off. Doolittle managed to land safely, but Cross bailed out and landed with his parachute in a cornfield full of sand burrs.

In Alaska, Cross was flying over tundra one day when his engine quit and he had to set down. He found that the fuel filter bowl was plugged with mosquitoes. He cleaned out the bowl and took off again no worse for the wear. Cross flew for Wien Airlines from 1936 to 1964. During this time, he started his own airline called Northern Cross Inc.

Cross was recalled to the army during World War II and stayed in the Reserve until retiring as a lieutenant colonel. He helped to cofound the Kotzebue Civil Air Patrol with Warren Thompson in the 1960s. He also owned the John Cross Trading Post with his second wife, who was one of the Magid family, and was active in politics of the territory and helped make Alaska a state. John Cross was a signer of the Alaskan Constitution.

In the book *The Last of the Bush Pilots*, a story is told how Cross was on his way down to Fairbanks. He had reported that he was having minor engine problems and then was not heard from. Among the searchers was Fred Goodwin, chief pilot for Wien Airlines, flying a new Cessna

Goddard native and Alaskan bush pilot John Milton Cross. *Courtesy of Alaska and Polar Region Collection and Archives, Elmer E. Rasmussen Library.*

195. The plane was so new that it was not known how it would handle deep snow landing on skis. Fred located John and attempted to land on four to five feet of snow. The plane was so heavy that it buried itself in the snow. When it stopped, only half of the plane was visible.

Now there were two pilots marooned on the Koyukuk River. It took several days to work a runway out in the snow with the help of another ski plane and some stomping with snowshoes. They finally flew both planes out, adding to the close calls that Cross had in his career.

Cross retired in the 1960s. On April 28, 1972, there was a Gathering of Eagles at the Elks Club Lodge in Cordova, Alaska. In attendance was the remainder of the old-time bush pilots, there to honor Merle K. "Mud Hole" Smith. Smith was the founder of Cordova Airlines and board member of Alaska Airlines.

John Milton Cross had two sons who were pilots: Milton, who logged more than one thousand hours in a helicopter in Vietnam, and Gordon, who was a captain for Wien Airlines. A third son, Harry, was a sergeant in the U.S. Air Force. His daughter, Susan, was a nurse.

KANSAS VOLCANO

Newspapers all over the nation carried the headlines: "Cracks in Earth Causing Worry." This story was datelined Anthony, Kansas, on August 22, 1911. The Kansas Geological Survey stated that there was no evidence of volcanic activity or actions in that area of the state. This author had not discovered why it was an accepted fact in 1911 that there was an old volcano in Harper County, Kansas. There is also an anomaly in the newspaper story that mentions Reno County. Following is the article that showed up in newspapers all over the nation:

Earth Splits Again in Kansas

Topeka KS: The old volcano that once sputtered and fumed in Harper County seems to be working again. Cracks two feet wide and of unknown depth have just opened in the earth to the north and east of the old volcano. The cracks appeared on two farms in Southeast Reno County, on the farm of J.M. Jorman and on the farm of Edward White. The earth simply parted, leaving the big cracks running for long distances across the fields.

The cracks appeared with a loud rumbling noise, similar to thunder. No one has ever seen the actual cracking, but many have seen the dust that arises and many have heard the noises accompanying the cracking.

The evidence of volcanic ash has been found in two locations in Harper County. Volcanic ash deposits have been found in many Kansas counties, and some have been mined. There was a large deposit in Pratt County that was mined for many years. Commercial mining of pearlite volcanic ash started in Harper County in the early part of the twentieth century from a pit one mile east of Anthony and was worked for many years by the Volco Company of Wichita. Later studies of the pit showed a layer of ash from two to six feet, although when Volco mined the pit the depth was reported at fifteen feet. A second ash deposit is known to be located in the county but has only been augered and not exposed. In Kingman County, there is a small deposit near St. Leo in the southwest part of the county.

In the record of earthquake activity by the Kansas Geological Survey, there is no record of an occurrence in the world on the date or year that the fields opened. The mention of Reno County in the article is still a mystery. There is also another strange happening that occurred in the area northwest of Harper and southern Kingman County in the 1960s near Spivey. The area six miles north and three quarters west of Attica was reported in the *Harper County Advocate* on February 7, 1963:

An area rabbit trapper heard a rumble and went to look at the area where dirt was shooting up in the air from a crack in the ground. The hole was estimated around seventeen feet in diameter when found. Later it expanded to fifty feet across and was spewing gas and dirt. On the following Friday the hole started to spew salt water. The state assistant of the Conservation Division of the Kansas Corporation Commission was notified. Initially it was thought to be surface gas or stray shallow gas that was released with the thawing of the ground. This theory was soon discarded. The eruption continued to belch gas, fresh and salt water from an extended depth. Around the area other holes and eruptions were taking place. One farmer counted two holes. The smaller holes soon slowed and stopped flowing. Oil operators in the area were checking their wells to see if any of the working and shut down wells were involved.

Salt water was flowing into Bluff Creek and was soon threatening area farmers and ranchers with contaminated water. Some farmers had to move their stock from the area. In an immediate circle around the eruptions were forty operating and abandoned oil wells. In the Spivey-Grabb Field, there were four hundred to five hundred wells.

John Roberts, state assistant of the Conservation Division, reasoned that it was unlikely that the "sudden volcano" had a base 4,500 feet down in the Mississippian strata formation that provided the oil and gas for the Spivey Field. He reasoned that a breech in a plugged well or pipeline could be causing the actions. Eventually, the eruption subsided. There is no record of determination of the cause.

MARION AND MAUDE FRAKES: MAUDE'S ROCK GARDEN

Although the whole community of Elk Falls knew that there was a rock garden at the old Frakes place, the rediscovery by Steve and Jane Fry revealed the garden when they purchased the property for their pottery operation. Overgrown and long abandoned, the garden is spurring new interest in who the builder was and why she built it.

The origins of the story go back to Marion Frakes, who was born in Indiana. How he ended up in Elk Falls, Kansas, may never be fully explained. Bits and pieces of the farm that Marion built and things that happened over the years don't paint the whole picture of who he was. We do know that he owned quite a bit of land in Elk County and that he employed up to four farmhands to help with his farming and cattle operation. The place is on the north side of Highway 160 at Elk Falls. It was built in 1897 and purchased by Marion in 1907. Having met a local Elk Falls girl who was teaching in Kansas City, Miss Maude Bird, Marion purchased many acres of land in Elk County that provided a base for the couple to make a living. The couple married in 1911.

A local man by the name of Clarence Sprague worked the farm and ranch until an unfortunate incident claimed the life of Mr. Sprague in an accident. Sprague had built a home near the "North Farm" of Marion's, and he was attempting to swim out to an island during a flood on the Elk River to drive several head of cattle back to safety. Over Marion's warnings not to attempt the swim, Sprague, who was a strong swimmer, made the attempt to drive the cattle anyway. The swift water overcame Mr. Sprague, and he drowned.

Marion died in 1930, and Maude carried on the business of running the farm and ranch. An advertising calendar that Marion put out listed him as a "cattle feeder and shipper." Whether as a hobby or as an artistic endeavor, Maude soon started on her rock garden. There are many sculptures and other things made from rock that Maude had built over the years, including a gazebo and an elephant that sprayed water, as well as many other elephants of all sizes. One piece she called a state monument because it contained a rock from every state in the Union.

Maude was quite passionate about Republican politics, hence the large number of elephants in the garden. She is listed as host of the Elk County Republicans meeting on September 14, 1936, in her "famous rock garden." The speaker was Mr. Willard Mayberry, who was part of the committee to elect Kansas governor Alf Landon as president of the United States. His speaking style was described as "speaking with wit, humor, guts, and his ability to hold the crowd's attention."

The Elk Falls musicians, directed by John McDiarmid, led the entertainment. The turnout was so great that two men had to direct the parking of cars. Maude's collection of elephants was displayed and received a lot of attention. One paper estimated the attendance at six hundred people.

Maude was very benevolent to the community, not only by hosting Republican events but also donating the hall to the Masonic Lodge. There were many other things she did that have gone unrecorded. For instance, she had a nephew stay with her quite a lot. As the lad, William Bird, grew up, she asked him to stay with her full time, and he became an important part of the ranch. At age sixteen, she asked his father for permission to adopt him, which she did. William adopted her last name and spent his life considering her to be a mother.

There was a dual purpose for the rock garden. Maude had an artistic side, certainly, but the times were also hard for many in the area. Farm prices were low during the Depression, so she hired local farmers to do the work of hauling rock and building the sculptures and structures for the garden. This gave them the opportunity for income and the dignity of work.

Maude died in 1954, and the house was closed. The property sat unattended, and vandals pretty much stripped the house. The house was almost relegated to a condition where it would be impossible to restore. That is, until 2004, when the Frys purchased the property. The pottery business is there today, and the garden is a work in progress.

The Frys have built a national reputation for their pottery work and had been in a studio in Elk Falls for many years. When they purchased the Frakes

Maude's elephants and rock garden. *Courtesy of Steve Fry.*

Elk Falls Pottery, Steve and Jane Fry. *Courtesy of Steve Fry.*

property, they knew that the work would be extensive, but it often turns out to be more work than bargained for. But the work was worth it, and visitors come to the Pottery Barn from all over the country. Because of the great pottery being produced, the Frys have become the keepers of a historic property that was saved from disappearing.

The Frys were instrumental in finding information about Maude and Marion and assisting with telling this story.

MASSEY HARRIS COMPANY: HUTCHINSON FACTORY

There was a lot of excitement in Hutchinson in 1924 with the prospects of leading farm manufacturer Massey Harris Company coming to look at sites and the region for the building of a factory for its line of combines. The country was just coming off a recession, and the advancement of farm machinery was starting to wind up and take off from where it was during World War I. With the drain on manpower during the war, there was a big push on labor-saving devices and becoming more efficient at food production.

Massey Harris Company started as two different companies in Canada, and when the two combined they became the leading producer of farm equipment in Canada. Soon the company was opening factories all over the world. One of those factories was the acquisition of the Johnston Harvester Company in Batavia, New York. An extension of operations from the Batavia plant started to look for locations to build in the middle of wheat country, where there was a large number of customers. It was also a convenient location for research and development of grain harvesters. Massey Harris's two main factories in the United States were Batavia, New York, and Racine, Wisconsin.

Hutchinson was calling itself the "Wheat Capital of Kansas," and it had a labor force and railway connections. The factory was built adjacent to the Santa Fe tracks between Lorraine Avenue and A Street, officially with an address of 1300 East Sherman. The factory was to assemble harvesters that were shipped in pieces by rail for assembly. The factory also housed an experimental division. Newspaper stories of the time told of Benton Massey coming to work the harvest with the factory team and witness the operations of the machines plus repair and work on improvements. The company

MASSEY-HARRIS "CLIPPER" COMBINE
POWER-TAKE-OFF DRIVEN — 6 FT. CUT

Massey Harris Clipper Combine, assembled in Hutchinson, Kansas. *Courtesy of* Antique Power Magazine.

policy was that family members learned the business from the ground up, including working in the hot Kansas harvest fields, before taking positions of importance in the organization.

The first shipment of Massey Harris combines was parked on side tracks, creating quite a sight and lots of comments. Thirty-four railcars were parked all over the area of the new factory. Motors were shipped in from Continental Motors in Detroit. The factory employed 150 workers and assembled twenty combines per week. In 1935, there was a major storm that hit the area, and the Massey Harris plant suffered a lot of roof and window damage. It took some time and expense to get everything back in order and into production again.

The Massey Harris plant had a large effect on the Hutchinson and Reno County economies and paid what was top wages for the time. The newspaper reported on the comings and goings of company officials. Local plant presidents and officials became part of the community. The wages were held up by one political candidate as an example of getting overall wages raised in the area.

Business was good when the factory was built, and an addition was added to the factory. The local paper published an estimate of Massey Harris's total worldwide size. The company made 275,000 machines per year that went to a total of sixty-nine international markets. The company made 2,009 types of machinery; the factories (total) covered more than six hundred acres. There were 7,500 worldwide employees. The most elaborate product was the harvester, with 9,810 parts. The simplest product was a jack with eight parts.

Locally, Massey Harris was sold by Reno Equipment. With the end of the 1920s and the beginning of the drought and Depression, many businesses could not stand the volatility of the business, and a number closed down. Massey Harris, with a net worth worldwide of $168 million in 1925, was able to withstand the downturn in the economy. The factory ran from 1925, and there was work done into the 1940s, although it is not specifically known what the last work in the factory was. The company introduced a successful self-propelled combine just before World War II. This made the pull-type combines assembled in Hutchinson obsolete.

During World War II, the Massey Harris Company sent the "Combine Brigade" from Texas through the Dakotas to harvest wheat while so many young men were away fighting the war. Food was one of the top priorities at this time. Today, Massey Harris, which became Massey Ferguson, is a part of AGCO, and the Massey Ferguson combine line is built in Hesston, Kansas.

OTTAWA MANUFACTURING COMPANY

As an old Kansas inventor, K.O. Huff, once said. "If you needed it and you could not afford to buy it, or it didn't exist, you built it." This was the ethic behind the Ottawa Manufacturing Company. It started out as an idea to simplify a daunting task and turned into a business that helped countless people. And it was all because of firewood.

At one time, the principal way of heating was by burning wood, which meant that wood had to be cut up and stockpiled to get through the winter. This task was done for many years by cutting down trees or taking downed trees and sawing the wood into sizes that would fit into fireplaces and stoves. The larger trunks and branches were often cut with a two-man saw and then split into workable pieces. It was a long, hard, time-consuming job that had to be done.

Farm families were always striving to find labor-saving methods to perform their farm work and other jobs in a faster, easier and more efficient way. In 1904, the Warner family consolidated several businesses into the Ottawa Manufacturing Company. One of those companies was the Warner Fence Company, which had invented and manufactured a woven fence wire that actually kept hogs in. It was an interlock style of wire and was used for many fencing applications.

The Warner Fence Company was started and located in two locations in Coffey County: Melvern and Waverly. Not far away, the Town of Ottawa was looking for businesses to improve the town. It started to court Warner Fence Company to move to Ottawa, but there were other towns trying to lure the company to their cities as well. Emporia was an active recruiter of the company, with its larger population and good rail connections. This prompted Ottawa to offer $3,000 to relocate, and the Warners took the offer. Both business locations were moved to Ottawa on King Street in North Ottawa in 1904.

The company started manufacturing hit-and-miss motors and had coupled a motor with a saw that would cut a log in two with no labor from a man other than setting up the saw and then letting the engine do the back-breaking work. The company was soon shipping twenty railcars of wire in from its supplier in Colorado per order. Into the line came more labor-saving devices and tools, from powered weed and grass cutters to windmills, power saws and post hole diggers. The engines were marketed under the name Union Foundry and Machine Company and also marketed directly to consumers under the name Warner.

Most of the engines were water-cooled hit-and-miss motors, but in 1915 the company marketed two models of an air-cooled engine. By 1917, there were fifteen models in its line. The Ottawa Crosscut Saw was sold in markets all over North America and became very popular. The company came up with a unique way of marketing products during World War I by accepting Liberty Bonds as payment because of the anti-German sentiment. The large German American communities were big purchasers of Liberty Bonds. The use of Liberty Bonds caused an inflationary period in 1919, and the value of the bonds dropped.

The company experienced a fire in 1917, which was a big blow to the company, but it continued through the 1920s and grew. In 1934, there was another fire. It again recovered and added to its product line, including filling station equipment and brake shoes for the railroads.

World War II brought challenges for the company. A janitor who worked in the 1920s had been picking up every nut, bolt and washer when sweeping up at night, and when the shortages of World War II hit, it was the barrels of these items that kept production going through the tough times. The

Ottawa Tree Saw. It revolutionized cutting up trees. *Author's collection, photo taken at Goessel Wheat Threshing Days.*

The Ottawa hit-and-miss engine. *Author's collection, photo taken at Goessel Wheat Threshing Days.*

government placed a large order for the saws, and they were put to work clearing airstrips and jungle bases.

The company started to manufacture a garden tractor named the Ottawa Mule Team Tractor—at least four models were built, along with a huge number of implements built for the tractors. Later models of the hit-and-miss motors carried the name of "The Ottawa."

The factory was flooded by the Marais des Cygnes River in 1951 and was never rebuilt.

SIDNEY TOLER: CHARLIE CHAN

When you start looking up information on actor Sidney Toler, there is very little said about his Kansas connections. He was born in Warrensburg, Missouri, on April 28, 1874, to parents Hooper G. and Sarah J. Toler. Hooper was a trotting horse trainer, but in the 1880s, the family moved to

Anthony, Kansas, where they ran a grocery store. They later on moved to Wichita, and newspaper articles list Sidney's father as a traveling salesman. Hooper owned a farm outside Wichita, however, and at one time owned a famous trotting horse named Ashen Wilkes, which was in the line of the greatest racehorse in the world, Dan Patch. Sidney's father then owned the Toler Theater in Wichita, which was managed by Foster, one of Sidney's brothers. Sidney had another brother, Edward, who was a dentist.

Sidney was active in plays at an early age and graduated from Wichita High School, moving on to the University of Kansas. He was active in local theater and worked as director, actor, playwright and theater director. He left KU, joined a theater group and toured for a number of years. Sidney ended up in New York on Broadway, where he worked with a host of future stars such as Helen Hayes, Edward G. Robinson, John Barrymore, Katharine Hepburn and Humphrey Bogart. He cowrote and directed *Golden Days*, staring Helen Hayes, and also cowrote and directed *The Exile* (1923), *Bye Bye Barbara* (1924) and *Ritzy* (1930).

After the stock market crash, Sidney moved to California and started playing bit parts in movies. His first Hollywood film was *Madam X*. When Warner Oland, the original actor playing Charlie Chan, died, there were thirty-four actors who auditioned to play the part. Sidney won that role and played it until his death from cancer in 1946.

The Charlie Chan franchise was a very lucrative and popular series based on six books by author Earl Derr Biggers that brought the Chan character to life. The series produced four dozen movies. The first four movies were not overly successful, and Fox cast Oland, a Swede, in the part; he was a big hit. As the second successful Charlie Chan, Toler labored up to his death. For the last three films he could barely walk. Midway through the series, the movies were filmed at Monogram Pictures, which put less money into production, yet the movies were still successful. There were six more films made after Toler's death before the series was ended.

Sidney is buried at Highland Cemetery in Wichita.

SKUNK JOHNSON

Many stories have been told about Skunk Johnson, and in the telling, the details have gotten a bit mixed up. Johnson was a trapper and buffalo hunter, and he came to the Pratt County area in 1872. Near the headwaters of the

Ninnescah River, he built into the side of a hill next to the river. The material was soapstone, which lent itself to sculpting out a very well-designed shelter that served him well.

Once Johnson went to Wichita for supplies, he was warned that the Indians were kicking up a ruckus and that he should be careful going back or not go at all. He was in the area where Kingman now stands when he noticed Indians following him. He realized that this band was seriously on the warpath, and he dropped his supplies and made a hair-raising escape, racing to reach his cave just before they caught up to him. He let his pony go and went in and threw up a barricade at the entrance.

As the Indians approached, he started to pick them off and shot quite a few. This enraged the Indians, and a siege began. The cave started into the hill and took a turn. Inside he had dug two chambers, one for sleeping and one for cooking. The cave had a spring inside, so he was not hurting for water. When frontal assaults continued to be costly, an effort was made to build a fire over his chimney and smoke him out. Then they tried to smoke him out by building a fire at his entrance, so he opened the chimney and pulled the smoke through. The siege lasted two weeks. During this time, he ran out of food, which had been the reason for the trip to Wichita in the first place, and he had dropped his supplies during the race. All he had left was skunk meat and oil. He had trapped skunks for the pelts. This is how his nickname came to be.

After losing several members of the war party over a two-week period, the siege ended and he was able to come out. Settlers started coming into the area, and the buffalo were being killed and driven farther west. Eventually, Johnson went to the Gunnison, Colorado area. His cave became a curiosity and for many years was used by local cowboys and travelers as shelter from the elements. The cave was also a retreat for freighters, and one time there were fifteen people taking shelter in the cave from a strong storm that held them up for three days. There were many inscriptions on the walls by those who used the cave over the years.

On February 4, 1911, Skunk got off the train at Stafford and was on his way to visit the old cave. The news was relayed to the *Wichita City Eagle*, which picked up the story of how he had lived off the meat of skunks to survive. He also wanted to see the inscriptions he had made on the walls, and sure enough, they were still there.

Skunk had spent the thirty-four years after living in the cave in the mountains and lived as a hermit. He made his living hunting and trapping. No mention was made as to why he was traveling east when he made his stop. Since Stafford is in the neighborhood of fifteen miles from the cave, he was apparently still in good health.

Local settlers noted that the fact that he trapped skunks for the fur, as well as everything else, meant he always had an "air" that announced his visit. He did not receive the moniker "Skunk" for this, but rather for surviving on skunk meat during the Indian siege, although it would not be a far reach to assume that his odiferous presence helped the name along.

THE GREEN TOP

Gene Miles, who was a home builder, put his office in an unusually designed building just west of Wichita (now it is located in Wichita) on Kellogg (US 54/400) at Lark Lane. On the corner just west of his office, he decided to develop a unique gas station with a restaurant and business space. Officially, it was called the Eclipse. It became known to everyone as the "Green Top," and for very good reason, it became a landmark.

The whole station complex was housed under a roof of curved laminated beams and was covered with green fiberglass panels. It certainly stood out on the side of the new highway, and it was a reference point to the neighborhood for years, even after it was torn down. Even on the hottest summer day, it seemed cooler under the roof. The gas station was leased to House Oil Company of Wichita. There was a small café that was noted for its Mexican food. For a short time on the south side of the building, there was a refrigerated box and parking for two Cream o'Gold Dairy trucks.

The station was built at this location because of the relocation of US 54 from Maple Street, or the "Old Cannonball," as it was known. Businesses started building west of Tyler Road because of the new highway project. The new four-lane changed the growth west of Wichita as the traffic increased and housing developments were built. New rapid growth consisted of motels, Blasi Oil Company and soon Doonan Truck and Horton's Furniture.

The August issue of *Practical Builder* did a feature story on the Green Top explaining the construction methods that were used with readily available materials. Four laminated beams that were eight by twenty inches created a one-hundred-foot span. On six-foot centers were four-by-sixteen-inch purlins fastened with steel hangers. To prevent lateral sway, there were crossties between the two-out beams. The south wall of the canopy consisted of steel I-beams with two-by-four-inch nailers. Reinforced green fiberglass panels were screwed on. The panels were in twelve-foot lengths and covered five thousand square feet of the gas station area. This kept the area free of rain and snow and made stopping much more of a pleasure than being in the wide open year-round.

The Kansas Gas & Electric Company consulted and worked with Miles on designing the lights and the all-electric café area. At night, the glow from the center could be seen for two miles. The cost of the entire project was $70,000. The design was intended to be a model for a wide variety of projects, such as supermarkets, warehouses and recreation centers. There was a patent pending on the center's design at the time the article was published.

The design at the time was described by the *Wichita Eagle & Beacon* as "the most modern gas station in the Wichita area and that it is the largest span of arches in the state." Many other publications did stories on the Eclipse, and motorists would stop and take pictures of it as they passed by. The location became a favorite stop in the area for carpools and buses.

By the end of the 1980s, there was deterioration setting in on the arches, and the canopy was torn down in 1990. The building was remodeled into a convenience store. The landmark status was gone, but it is still referred to by the old-timers as the "Green Top corner." The highway has been rebuilt and a new interchange placed at Maize Road, and the city limits of Wichita now extend west to Colwich Road, meeting the Goddard city limits.

TRAGIC HAPPENING ON THE NINNESCAH

In the Great Flood of 1923, a tragedy on the Ninnescah River became one of those stories that get passed around—many years later, the details are lost and it becomes legend. South of Garden Plain about nine miles and on the south side of the South Fork of the Ninnescah River, there was a four-square home that was not far from the riverbank. This was the home of the Renner family. The joining of the North Fork and South Fork of the Ninnescah is within a half mile.

The rivers are famous for flooding over the years, and where the two rivers meet, water can back up and can reach three miles wide. Water has been known to reach within eyesight of the town of Cheney, which is upstream roughly five miles. The rivers are typically a shifting sand river and, throughout history, have wandered back and forth across the floodplain. The building of the Cheney Dam and Reservoir has reduced the number and severity of floods since the 1960s, but there can still be bad flooding from Pratt to Mulvane.

On June 28, 1923, the rain had been coming steadily for a night and a day. Flooding was beginning in the lowest portions of the floodplain, and it was visible from the Renners' house. The house sat next to the mile line, and it had never had a bridge at this location, only a ford. The bridge was a half mile south and a half mile east.

The Renners had four girls and five boys, one boy being a ten-and-a-half-month-old baby. The family said their prayers and went to bed. When the mother awakened the kids, there was about three inches of water in the house. In the yard, there was a three-legged windmill. Mr. Renner quickly broke up tables in the house for boards to place on the windmill for the family to scramble up onto to stay out of the water. The water kept rising, and by the time the family made it to the windmill, the water was almost over their heads.

They got settled on the windmill and soon could not see any land around them. The thunder and lightning made for a long night, and everyone was anxious. There was a gate that hooked to the windmill. Mr. Renner went down to check on things and found that one leg was being washed out. The windmill was in danger of collapse, but it was too late. He frantically tried to get the gate open so the debris would not build up. The windmill started going down, and it was a scramble to get everyone up on the folded-over tower. In the meantime, Mr. Renner's leg was caught while he was struggling with the gate.

Mrs. Renner was holding the baby in a blanket and was frantically trying to stay on the tower and find her husband, who she thought was drowning. In all the scramble and surging water, the baby slipped out of the blankets, and there was a panic trying to find him. The water started going down, and the family made it back to the house, which was full of mud. As the sun came up, Mrs. Renner cried out upon seeing the baby's body, floating and stuck on the barbed wire fence. Mr. Renner retrieved the body, brought it back into the house and laid it on a table.

There was nothing to do but walk out of the area to an uncle's home three miles away. As they walked through the water for about a mile and a half, there were several other families who came to the large home for refuge. The men walked back to the house to retrieve the body of the drowned infant. Mr. Renner and another man took the baby to town to get a coffin and make arrangements for a funeral. The trip to Garden Plain involved a relay in order to get there. Two bridge approaches along the way were washed out. They had to drive to the bridge, climb up and walk over. Then they went to the next bridge and did the same thing. Finally arriving at Garden Plain, the funeral was held at St. Anthony's Catholic Church, with the burial in the church cemetery.

When I first researched this story, all I had to go on were coffeeshop stories. There is nothing remaining where this tragedy occurred. The right-of-way crossing and the road have been abandoned. After much digging and asking questions, I found a family name. I was fortunate enough to find a relative who had been transcribing a diary and was able to get the family story in full. There is a small headstone for the baby in the cemetery in Garden Plain, and there are still a number of family members who live nearby. Many had never heard the story before or had only heard bits and pieces.

Ten-and-a-half-month-old Marion Renner lies at peace near some cedar trees at the St. Anthony Aleppo Cemetery in Garden Plain.

TWIN WINDMILL COMPANY

Give a farmer a problem and soon there will be dozens of thinkers and tinkerers coming up with solutions to the problem. Kansans seem to have a built-in genetic quality to dream and build. It goes back to the old saying "Necessity is the mother of invention."

There were two things in Kansas that when combined would inspire invention and industry: the need for water and the constant wind. Once people started moving away from water sources on the vast prairies, there was a need for water. When the railroads were built, two things influenced routes. One was the need to create a revenue stream. Hauling settlers and materials out on the plains was not a profitable venture if there was not something to haul back. So there was a need for settlers to produce goods as much as a need for them to buy goods. Also, the train engines were steam driven, so a reliable source of water was necessary.

With the abundance of wind, it was natural to take the principles of turning a windmill to pump water and bring it up for stock, crops and power. There were many companies and individuals designing windmills and manufacturing them in the state and all over the country. One of the most unusual designs was from the Twin Windmill Company of Hutchinson, Kansas.

The Twin Windmill, manufactured in Hutchinson, Kansas. *Courtesy of the American Wind Power Museum, Lubbock, Texas.*

Albert F. George of Garden City designed the Twin Windmill and filed for a patent on June 29, 1914. Although the patent was received on December 30, 1919, the first Twin Windmill was manufactured in 1917. The production continued until 1927 or 1928. The factory in Hutchinson was later used by Marriage Combine to build his first self-propelled tractor thresher. The plant later became the headquarters for Krause Manufacturing.

The only known example of a restored and operational Twin Windmill is in the American Wind Power Museum in Lubbock, Texas. The windmill was retrieved from a farm in Washington State. It is fully restored and functioning as a display piece. The reason for the twin mill was for power. The mill was designed as an irrigation unit. The pump that the mill had was designed to pump two hundred gallons per minute. The company explained the device:

> No time or money has been spared to perfect this wonderful windmill. It is built of the best selected metals used in like constructions, and there is not a particle of wood about the windmill to deteriorate or decay. The mill works on a solid chrome alloy steel ball turntable. It has only about half the bearings of the ordinary windmill and is as near frictionless as it seems possible to construct a windmill. It has no gearing whatever. Has a solid steel roller chain drive. Our customers say it pumps ten times the water of an ordinary windmill. We have customers that have been using our windmills for years, some of them operating them from three to four mills, and they are, as far as we know, all of one accord in pronouncing it the most practical irrigator in existence.

It is noteworthy that later on, the company had trouble with the chains breaking and converted the newer versions into a geared design. Of all the windmills produced in Kansas, the Twin Wheel has to be the most interesting.

U.S. GUYER

Ulysses Samuel Guyer was born at Paw Paw, Lee County, Illinois, on December 13, 1868, to a family of seven siblings. His father, Joseph, was a Brethren preacher and started or pastored churches everywhere the family lived. Leaving Paw Paw, the family moved to Grundy, Iowa. In 1875, they moved six miles south of Sterling, Kansas, just in Reno County. In 1880, they moved to Bazaar and then, in 1881, to El Dorado, where they lived six miles east. In 1883, they moved to Lincoln Township near Furley and owned the first farm that the railroad came through when it headed to Wichita for the Rock Island. In 1893, the family traded for a farm between Stafford and St. John. Here is where his father died, after a horse kicked him. U.S. Guyer came home from his studies to take care of the family estate. Around this time, the principal at St. John High School, James Brady, died, and Guyer was asked to fill his term. He stayed as principal and superintendent for five years.

Guyer then attended school at Lane University in Lecompton, Southwest Business College in Wichita, Western College, Coe College and the University of Kansas. He held degrees from Western College, Coe College and the Kansas City School of Law. He went to Kansas City to practice law in 1901; he was elected judge of the First Division City Court in 1907 and then mayor of Kansas City, Kansas, in 1909. He was appointed to fill the term of Congressman Edward C. Little, who died in office, for 1924 and 1925. He did not run for the following term, but he did run and was elected in 1927, staying in Congress until he died on June 6, 1943.

It is noted that he was appointed to conduct the impeachment panel against Judge Harold Louderback of the District Court for the Northern District of California. Another committee that Guyer served on has largely escaped the scrutiny of history, and there is no mention in most articles of his service: the attempted *coup d'état* of President Franklin Roosevelt.

There had been a plot by several large industrialists, bankers and others to attempt to remove President Roosevelt. The group attempted to persuade one of the best-known Marine Corps generals to be its leader in removing the president. The general played along long enough to uncover their plans and then brought the plan to the attention of the government. The "Business Plot," as it was called, occurred in 1933. At the time, the news media dismissed the plot as a gigantic hoax. Retired Marine Corps major general Smedley Butler testified before the United States House of Representatives Special Committee on Un-American Activities (the McCormack-Dickstein Committee) on these claims. The conspiracy was trying to get General Butler to become head of a fascist veterans organization in a coup to overthrow Roosevelt, due to the unrest from the veterans demanding the bonus that was voted for them in Congress and which they never received—they were known as the "Bonus Army."

U.S. Guyer, St. John, Kansas. Principal of St. John High School, lawyer and Kansas congressman. *Courtesy of Stafford County Historical Museum.*

In the book *The Plot to Seize the White House* by Jules Archer, conservative financiers were horrified and concerned over the gold standard. Roosevelt was damned as a Socialist or Communist and was feared to be out to destroy private enterprise. All those implicated in the plot denied that they had tried to lure General Butler into it. Roosevelt had been warned of something similar to this by William Dodd, the U.S. ambassador to Germany. Long after the fact, it was discovered that Representative Samuel Dickstein had been paid by the Russian KGB the entire time the committee was in session. The matter just went away.

U.S. Guyer remained single until late in life, when he married Alice Dougherty of Yankton, South Dakota. They had been engaged for twenty-two years. Guyer died in Bethesda, Maryland, on June 5, 1943, and is buried at the Fairview Cemetery in St. John, Kansas.

VIOLA SPRINGS WATER: CHARLES G. DAVIS

Charles G. Davis was the eldest son of Cottonwood Davis, and he spent time running the farm in Viola Township, the first organized township in Sedgwick County. The Davis family was the first to settle there and built the first frame house. The farm was located at the north end of Viola Township at the location today of what is 71st Street South and 263rd Street West (Viola Road). The farm was located on Clear Creek and just north of the Ninnescah River, just downstream from where the North and South Forks come together. It is a sandy-type soil, and the farm had eight springs on it that ran clear and pure. In fact, the water was so pure that the State of Kansas tested it and found it free of bacteria and just less than 100 percent pure. The water ran higher in quality than the famous Colorado Springs Water and Eureka Springs Water. With such a pure water source, a cement bottling plant was built on the farm, and Viola Springs Water was delivered to Wichita and surrounding communities. The product was in very high demand, especially when there was an outbreak of cholera in Wichita, as well as another outbreak in Wellington. Viola Springs Water was the first company delivering bottled water in the region but was soon followed by a healthy competition from Conway Springs Water Company.

There was a flood in the area around 1915 when torrential downpours swelled all the creeks and the rivers in the area. A few miles upstream from the farm there was a manmade lake on Clear Creek owned by several prominent families from Wichita. The earthen dam and flow control box washed out under the stress of the huge amounts of water it was trying to hold back. The dam burst, and the wave that went downstream caused considerable damage to the Davis farm, killing many animals and doing property damage. Davis brought a lawsuit against the owners that was in litigation for years. Evidence suggests that the suit eventually failed, and Davis did not receive any compensation for the damage.

The Viola Water Company offices were located in Wichita, and delivery routes were centered there. The spring water was bottled directly from the source on the farm into glass bottles. At first, it was hauled to Wichita by horse and wagon, later by motorized trucks. The last known location of the office was 1427 West Douglas. City business directories show the company at this address in 1920. In the 1923 directory, the company was not shown at this address, and it had become Vinton & Boren Auto Repair Shop.

In 1920, a Dr. Nyberg declared that the water from Viola Springs and Conway Springs was contaminated and that the process of shipping the water from the source and rebottling it was likely the cause. In a rebuttal to the statement, Davis stated that the water is bottled directly at the farm in the plant and is never diverted through pipes or rebottled. The bottling plant was inspected and approved by the State of Kansas. Any contamination that the doctor found was never found by state inspectors.

Between 1920 and 1923, mention of the company diminished and advertising dropped off. Nothing has been found to explain what happened to the company. In 1920, Davis was quoted as supporting a county-owned ice plant. At the time, the ice company that served the area was thought to be too expensive.

In the *Wichita Beacon* of January 28, 1923, a map and story were run on a proposed waterline to be run from Viola Springs to Wichita for the purpose of selling water to the Wichita Water Department. At the time, the piping of water from Mission Springs Water, west of Newton, was estimated to cost $6 million. If the city had gone with the Davis proposal, it would have cut the pipeline length in half.

In 1922, C.G. Davis penned a historical article for the *Wichita Beacon* on telephone lines and railroads. The Union Pacific Railway was discussed as the first in Kansas running from Wyandotte County to Lawrence. This became known as the Eastern Division. His late father was the general roads agent at that time. The last mention of Davis came in an endorsement for Doan's Pills.

What happened to the farm? It is now YMCA Camp Hyde. The property was eventually purchased by A.H. Hyde and family. Mr. Hyde was a great supporter of the YMCA, and the camp had been formed and given to the organization in the 1950s. It has extensive facilities, lakes and a very clear swimming pool.

VOLCO MANUFACTURING COMPANY

"CLEANLINESS—PURITY—HEALTH—USE VOLCO!" This was the motto on an advertisement for Volco Cleanser in a 1912 *Wichita Beacon* newspaper ad. These ads ran in papers all over the country from the early 1900s until 1923. The company history includes a story about a naturally occurring substance contained in what most thought was just waste ground but which turned out to be a gold mine of a raw material. This was during the time that science was just discovering that germs were unhealthy and when the chance discovery of a deposit of volcanic ash near Anthony turned into a business.

C.E. McCready was a successful associate with the Prudential Insurance Company and was making a sales call near Anthony one day. Just east of town, there was an area of white ground that did not raise anything, and local farmers just considered it waste ground. McCready took a notion that this was possibly a valuable deposit of volcanic ash and had a sample tested. According to the news reports of the time, the worthless white soil was actually one of the only known pure volcanic ash deposits of its kind in the United States.

There were two tracts of the ash near each other just to the east of the Anthony city limits. McCready was fascinated by the raw substance that, when applied to the back of his watch, would shine it up like new. The polishing never left a scratch on what it was cleaning. He could just imagine the possibilities of the use of the substance. He immediately acquired the land and started to negotiate with local businessmen in Wichita to form a corporation to mine and produce cleaning and polishing products from the ash.

Samples were sent to the U.S. Geological Survey for analysis, and the ash was pronounced a very valuable substance. The USGS did not believe that any deposits were known in the country of this purity and type. Incorporation took place, and McCready was voted president.

Many prominent men of the time in Kansas became investors in the $300,000 corporation. Harry Walker, who was active in business at the time in Wichita, purchased a large block of stock and was named assistant manager. Also on the board of directors was William T. Benson, president of the Ranchman's State Bank. Judge John Madden, one of the Midwest's leading lawyers, was also a stockholder and on the board.

According to the general manager of Volco, the vein of volcanic ash was fifteen feet thick; at a yield of fifty tons per day, mining the deposit would last 115 years. There was a railroad spur built to the site, and all raw material was shipped by railcar to the plant in Wichita for processing into soap, house cleaning preparations, polish for windows, mirrors and other products.

The quality of the products was so high that an analysis of the cleanser by a comparison report prepared by G.A. Bragg put the moisture at 1.85 percent, soap at 3.69 percent and volcanic ash at 93.51 percent. That made this product the purest with the fewest components of those studied. Twenty-three different products were compared in the study.

Products made by Volco were packaged in cans that were manufactured in Wichita and distributed across the country. At one point, a contract was won to sell product to all institutions owned by the State of Kansas. Sales offices were established in Topeka and Salina, as well as other points around the country. Ads were placed in papers soliciting women to sell the Volco products door to door in their area.

At one point, a lawsuit was brought against several railroads in an attempt to lower the cost of shipping. At some point in 1922, there were some problems in the company, and a creditor asked for the company to be placed into receivership. One shareholder also asked that the company be adjudicated by the court to appoint a receiver for the company. Finley P. Miles, who was a shareholder with twenty-two shares in Volco, filed suit, stating that while the company was not insolvent, the liabilities that were accumulating against the company were not being paid.

Harry M. Washington filed suit in district court alleging that Volco had owed him $1,313.30 for services rendered when making an audit of the company. A receiver was appointed for the company. At that time, the appraisers fixed the assets of the Volco Company at $515,000, although assets included an estimated 504,410 tons of volcanic ash on the property at Anthony in Harper County. Value on the ash was set at $2.95 per ton. Total value of assets included inventory, supplies and accounts receivable but did not take into account the value of "goodwill" or the formulas of the compounds.

For all that can be determined, the company was closed in 1923. Products were still being advertised on store shelves in 1924, but the Volco name disappeared from all news after this point. It is not known where C.E. McCready went or what business he was in after this point. The same name comes up all over the country involved in timber, lumber and other companies, but there are no ties that can be found to prove that any of these were the same man.

Bentonite was discovered on the property where the volcanic ash was located in Harper County, but there is no information if it was mined or exploited. An article in the *Anthony Republican* in 1926 noted that a "Volco factory would be built on the site of the volcanic ash deposits." This Volco plant was owned by Volcanic Ash Company of America, a Missouri-based company. There is no record of how this company acquired ownership of the deposits near Anthony or if there was any connection with C.E. McCready.

THE VOLCO MFG. CO.

Will put on their

First Selling Campaign in Wichita

Commencing Monday, March 8,

Continuing 30 Days.

This will be put on under the auspices of the different church societies of the city. A liberal commission given to these societies.

25 societies in Topeka last month participated in our big selling in that city where about two carloads of Volco were sold.
Presidents of societies call, or phone at once for information.

J. A. HOPKINS, Sales Mgr.
Phone M. 510   VOLCO MFG. CO.   402 Schweiter Bldg.

Volco Manufacturing advertisement. *Wichita Eagle*, February 28, 1914. *Courtesy of Newspapers.com.*

At the same time, there was a listing of a Volco Company in New York State, but there are no obvious connections. The Volcanic Ash Company of America also acquired a deposit of ash near Meade and ran a rail spur to the site to transport the raw materials to its facilities.

The factory for the Volco Company was located at 138 North Wichita Street. The Kansas Gas & Electric Company leased the brick building after the assets of Volco were dispersed. The owner of the building, listed as Miss Elisabeth Kimball, was a woman from Philadelphia, Pennsylvania. There is no information on how she was owner of the building at this time. The building was three stories and 50 by 140 feet in dimension.

The deposit of volcanic ash is a mystery. A pit was mined in Pratt County as well as Meade County over the years, and the Kansas Geological Survey lists several locations in Kansas with ash deposits. It is one more piece of a puzzle regarding the news reports of an old volcano in Harper County and at least two events of earth splitting and steam, ash and water coming from the ground at two points in state history. According to the Kansas State Geological Survey, there is no sign of an old volcano in the state.

W.A. DYE CHILI, WICHITA

In 1919, a newspaper article called Dye's Chili Mixture, which was made in Wichita, "the mixture that fed the boys in France giving them 'pep' that helped them win the war." The same article credited Dye's Chili with giving the boys the "steel to win the war." The Dye label remained the same over its forty-year span. The logos of the Chili Kid and the Chili Kids were designed by local artist and Prairie print maker C.A. Seward (1884–1939). The Chili Kid was a Hispanic boy holding a large bowl of chili in one hand and a large spoon in the other.

W.A. Dye began his career in the food industry as a grocer in 1898. By 1907, he had begun the very successful business manufacturing chili and sold it to operators of chili stands. After World War I, the business expanded, and he built a two-story building, hiring local architect Glenn H. Thomas for the design. The building at 120 North Mosley Street in Wichita had the letters "DYE" etched in a limestone lintel over the front door and had his name etched on all of the original windows.

W.A. Dye Chili mixture advertisement, featuring the Chili Kid. *Wichita Beacon*, April 30, 1919. *Courtesy of Newspapers.com.*

Dye's Chili products were shipped throughout the United States, Canada, Mexico, South America, Australia and New Zealand. Dye became known as the "chili center for the western half of the U.S." Most of the advertising was by word of mouth, but many newspaper ads have been found featuring the Chili Kid and the Chili Kids.

One of the most common newspaper ads reads:

> *I am the Chili Kid, Known by Good Chili Makers Everywhere. Write to me for prices and information regarding the chili business. Dye's Chile Mixture contains everything but the meat and beans for making the genuine article.*
>
> *10¢ and 25¢ at All Grocers. W.A. Dye Chili Supplies, Wichita Kansas.*

The second ad features the same figure, only smaller, and six of them in a row. The label reads:

> *Dye's Chile Kids. See how happy these Dye's Chile kids are. Your children too will like chili if you make it from Dye's Chile Mixture. The grownups like it also, and it's so easy to make. In handy shake containers, 15¢ and 35¢ sizes. Recipe book free. "Always say Dye's." At all good grocers DYE'S CHILI MIXTURE made by W.A. Dye. Everything in chili supplies. Wichita Kansas.*

Dye wanted to keep his business small and employed no more than seven or eight people. Also important, Dye did not want to can his product. Wichita's Continental Can Company moved to Denver and began canning Ellis Chili, which was made more readily available and gained national recognition. But loyal customers knew that bigger did not mean better.

After the design of the company logo, leaflets were made and dropped off at chili shops. The product was eventually put into cans, which made the chili mix more available. The chili was served in scores of chili parlors and at ice cream stands, peanut stands, church socials and restaurants.

When W.A. Dye passed away, the company was inherited by his son. In 1966, he sold it to his attorney's son and a group of high school friends. Within two years they had closed the business because new OSHA requirements were cost-prohibitive for the plant.

WALKER FAMILY INVENTIONS

Anyone who is knowledgeable about commercial turf or lawn mowers is familiar with the name Walker. It is true that today the mowers are manufactured in Colorado, but the Walkers' roots are in Kansas. Max Walker farmed in the Fowler area, was quite handy building things and had an idea to build a special Christmas present for his son Bob. Bob was seven years old and had a dream. Bob loved Caterpillar tractors, so Max decided to build a miniature Caterpillar for him. It took many hours before a pedal-powered Caterpillar dozer was built in the farm shop. The gift was well loved by all the Walker kids: Bob, Ruth, Dean and Nina. The kids put the dozer to heavy-duty playtime use and proved the quality of Max's design and engineering. Later on, the pedals were replaced with a small engine.

Max was a fan of tracked equipment, and his invention of the Power Track received a lot of interest. It was shown at the Kansas State Fair in the late 1950s. It prompted thoughts of turning it into a business. There were limits on the tools and not a lot of capital to invest, plus he was still a full-time farmer. But his talents would not be shelved for long.

A friend of Max's told him that a gasoline-powered golf car would be very practical since golf carts of the time would not always make a full round of golf without the batteries going down. His interest piqued, he went into the shop and designed the Walker Executive Golf Car. The three-wheeled golf car was more than a golf cart. Being a farmer, Max used many components that came straight from farm machinery and were built bull strong. The car had a desirable feature in that the body would tilt up so it was easy to work on. Part of the ruggedness was the actual tractor and farm components used.

The golf car was a hit. Manufacturing was limited in the farm shop, so a brand-new forty-by-eighty-foot factory was built on the farm. The design was imitated by several manufacturers, but they did not solve some of the critical components of the car. As batteries got better and more feasible, the design was sold to a group of investors in Salina. About one thousand golf cars were made.

The Walker Executive Golf Car was a seasonal product and considered to be a narrow market, so the Power Truck was designed and built. It was a true runabout that was more for industry, to be used inside factories; also some were used for mail delivery and even pizza delivery. It was used as a floor scrubber in factories and even used on decks of aircraft carriers. Son Dean could be seen zipping around Fowler in his little Power Truck.

The first Walker dozer. First built for a Christmas present, it was later motorized and sold. *Courtesy of Walker Manufacturing Company.*

Financial limitations and lack of suppliers forced the company to move out of Kansas. The company went to Casper, Wyoming, and was sold to investors. Max stayed on as an employee, not having ties to ownership or management. The new owners did not do well, and the company closed after a few years.

Working as a welder in Casper, Wyoming, Max was approached by a Greeley, Colorado company, Byco, to develop an agricultural cab cooler. After designing the cab cooler, Max was able to raise enough money to buy back the assets of the company. Byco gave him a contract to build the coolers. Son Dean came up to help, and they set up shop in an old bakery. Byco persuaded Max that they should be located near its factory in Fort Collins, Colorado. Bob joined the company that year. Although the coolers were moving, they were not that profitable.

The development of the mowers began in 1977. The mower became the mainline of the company. By 1996, the company's dealers and customers had grown, and the 25,000[th] mower came off the line. Mowers and decks were built separately and by 2008, the 100,000[th] mower and deck were built.

On September 19, 2011, Wesley "Max" Walker passed on. He left a legacy of innovation and hard work. The company is still a leader in the lawn and turf industry. Although we wish it were a Kansas company again, it is still the story of an imaginative Kansan who had ideas and turned them into reality.

WICHITA TRACTOR

In the second decade of the twentieth century, there was a growing need for lightweight tractors and machinery to start the process of replacing the horse on the farm. The need for huge steam or heavyweight traction engines was limited due to the fact that most of the sod that was going to be farmed had already been broken out, and the cost of these behemoths was too much for 160-acre farms. The average size of farms at the time was 160 to 320 acres because of preemption in the early settlement period.

Kansas was a hotbed of invention and dreams of building industry, and as much or more effort went into the invention of farm equipment as did the aircraft that captured so many imaginations. Wichita had aspirations of being a major player in the manufacture of traction engines, and a frantic effort was made in building and selling tractors.

Originally the National Tractor Manufacturing Company, chartered on September 29, 1916, the company had already merged with another group and renamed the Wichita Tractor Corporation on March 22, 1917. The company produced two lightweight tractors under the name and model Wichita Tractor, one being 8-16, and also under the name Midwest 9-18—the second designation coming after yet another re-incorporation under the name Agrimotor Tractor Company.

The timeline and mergers are hard to decipher, as there were separate companies joining together and manufacturing tractors. Wichita Tractor was located at 421 North Water in Wichita from 1917 until 1920. The Midwest tractor was produced until the dissolution of the company.

The tractors were powered by a Giles two-cylinder opposed engine with a five-by-six-and-a-half-inch bore and stroke. The tractor weighed 3,300 pounds and sold for $1,085. It had a Kingston carburetor, Bennett air cleaner and Atwater-Kent ignition.

As noted in a 1920 *Wichita Beacon* story, "The Agrimotor Company recently incorporated for $125,000 has completed its plans for reorganization and establishing of a manufacturing plant in this city. The new organization consolidated with the Wichita Tractor Company, taking over entire holdings of that company, temporary offices at 421 N. Water on the premises formerly occupied by the Wichita Tractor Company." The board president was listed as C.W. Lewis.

There was an announcement in a trade publication that the Agrimotor Company was building a new two-story plant in Joplin, Missouri, at Ninth and Illinois. The 1921 Joplin City Directory lists the Agrimotor Company at 121 Miners Bank Building and lists C.W. Lewis as president. By the following year, at the same address but a different listing, the company had changed to the Auto Metal Bearing Company. The last mention in any trade magazine about the tractor or equipment was 1924.

The Kansas charter for the Agrimotor Company was abandoned on September 24, 1922. It is not known how many Wichita or Midwest tractors were manufactured and sold. One was found in 2014 and sold at auction

The Finest Tractor of Them All

The Wichita Tractor, newspaper advertisement. *Wichita Beacon*, June 23, 1917. *Courtesy of Newspapers.com.*

near Wichita. It was confusing when starting out to piece together the history of the company. At the same time, there was a Royer Tractor built in Wichita not far from the Wichita Tractor Company's factory. The Royer is another story.

The rush to build tractors during this time also reflects the increasing demand for agricultural products because of the raging war in Europe and the need to feed a hungry Europe. Huge numbers of horses were purchased by the British government for use in the war. During the years 1917 and 1918, a large number of young men, many farm workers, were required for military service. There was also the great loss of life from the influenza epidemic. Many companies suffered the immediate depression from 1920 to 1922, and a great many mergers and company bankruptcies changed the landscape of agriculture.

WICHITA: BROOM CORN CAPITAL

Wichita has been known by several titles, from "Peerless Princess of the Plains" to the "Air Capital of the World," but once it was known as the "Broom Corn Capital of the World." At the turn of the twentieth century, one of the major agricultural crops was broom corn. As its name suggests, the straw of broom corn was used to make brooms. Even with all the innovations over the years, a broom can be found in most every home and business today.

The first industry in Pratt, Kansas, was a broom company owned by William Bergen. Bergen raised all of his own broom corn for his broom factory and employed many local people. But Wichita had the distinction of beating Chicago as the broom corn capital. In a newspaper article in the *Wichita Daily Eagle* of October 3, 1920, the city had five hundred buyers in the city who came from all parts of the United States, Cuba, Mexico and other countries. The article stated that $800,000 worth of brush was handled by the corn dealers of the city.

Of the companies making brooms in Wichita, one of the biggest was the Southwestern Broom Manufacturing Company. The company was based in Evansville, Indiana, and it built a factory adjacent to the railroad tracks at the corner of Fifteenth and Santa Fe. This building was built in 1908, after the company had been in Wichita for twenty years (since 1888), and was north of the Otto Weiss Alfalfa Mill, near the stockyards.

A building 200 by 260 feet was constructed. The building was four stories tall and cost $35,000.

Southwestern Broom was started by August Rosenberger, who was a grocer in Evansville, Indiana. One customer, a farmer, could not make ends meet or pay his grocery bill. The farmer offered a broom-making machine, sewing machine and a small shack. Mr. Rosenberger wished the man well, sending him on his way. It was not in Mr. Rosenberger's nature to own something that was not being used and so started making brooms. The business soon took off, and he sold his grocery store to his partner. The production of brooms grew to the point that it made sense to move to the marketplace, so he moved to Wichita. There he built a factory and called it Southwestern Broom and Warehouse Company.

In 1907, Rosenberger created the Atlantic Broom Company, purchasing the inventory and contracts of the Calvert Broom and Brush Company. Eventually, the company closed operations in Wichita and did business from Baltimore, Maryland, changing its name to the Atlantic-Southwestern Broom and Brush Company. This business closed in 1989 after 101 years in business.

One of the broom products advertised by Southwestern Broom in 1919 was the "Little Lady Broom." The ad claimed that they were the "World's largest broom makers, Wichita."

In 1912, Wichita sold sixty-five thousand tons of broom corn. The industry had eighteen companies, 20 brokers and 176 traveling men who covered the area buying the products in the field. There was a lot of raw material exported to other countries and locations. The price in 1911 reached $215 per ton, an all-time high. A lot of broom corn was raised in the panhandles of Oklahoma and Texas, as well as New Mexico. The total value of the crop from 1892 to 1911 was $12,962,287.

The industry dwindled with the introduction of alternative materials, but there are still corn brooms that can be bought everywhere. Now airplanes, wheat, cattle and other crops overshadow broom corn in the state, but at one time, it was the base for prosperity on the plains.

SUPREME PROPELLERS

Aircraft have played such a huge role in the history of Kansas that it is natural to have component companies spring up to support the fascination of Kansans—and the world—with flight. The 1920s were a booming time, and prospects seemed to have no end in sight. Since Wichita was earning the name "Air Capital of the World," it drew many who would contribute to the industry.

Morris J. "Pop" Stone was one who came to Wichita. Starting in Washington, D.C., in 1910, Pop Stone started the Excelsior Propeller Company. He moved the company in 1912 to St. Louis, Missouri, where, according to the company brochure, he earned the confidence of all the leading aviators and aeronautical exhibition companies then in existence by designing and manufacturing the most efficient and most beautiful propellers in the United States.

In 1917, with the entrance of the United States into World War I, the company was reorganized as the Stone Propeller Company and moved to Dayton, Ohio. At Dayton was McCook Field, which was the U.S. government's Aviation Experimental Station. The company manufactured propellers for Liberty, Hispano-Suiza, Rolls-Royce, Curtiss, Hall-Scott, Gnome, Le Rhône and many other motor companies. The company also manufactured a large number of propellers that were used on the De Havilland 4 combat planes.

The company moved to Wichita in 1928, starting production at 1016 South Santa Fe. Later that year, the company built the world's largest wooden propeller factory at 915 East Lincoln. This is where Lincoln and Washington are today. It is listed that the company was run by Stone and his four sons; the company is now called the Supreme Propeller Company.

Supreme lasted until 1930, when it closed due to the Depression. Pop Stone returned for a short time in 1934. A great-grandson related the story of Pop Stone and offered some insight into the life he lived. He described his great-grandfather as something of a "gypsy," born in England and moving to the United States in the early 1900s. His experience was not with airplane props but with ship propellers. He became enamored of the aircraft industry and started Stone Manufacturing. Stone was a friend of the Wright brothers, who were frequent guests at the Stone home.

Stone went broke after both world wars because he geared up for too much production for government contracts, and the government cut its contracts after the wars. This left him holding large amounts of supplies and material. In the late 1940s, some people in Chicago set him up in business. The family believes that some of those investors were gangsters. The company received a contract for a large order for Piper, and the partners wanted him to cut corners. Not wanting the responsibility for that, he changed the pitch of the props so they would not generate enough thrust to get the planes off the ground. He then skipped town, ending up in Grand Rapids, Michigan, where he went into business for the last time. It is noted that the bad props were "not airworthy."

Of the more than eighty aircraft companies in existence in the 1920s, fifty-three of them were in Wichita. This gave Wichita the rightful name "Air Capital of the World," and it seems natural that so many component companies would locate there. At the time, the aircraft industry could be likened to the Wild West. Just as the West has matured, so has the aircraft industry.

PELICAN PETE: ELIAS PELTON

A large man with a fiery red beard, something in his demeanor made the name Pelican Pete very appropriate. A hermit with peculiar habits and an immense appetite made him a character everyone knew in the Stafford County area. The Stafford County Museum compares this real-life character to Johnny Appleseed and Paul Bunyan. The stories about this man rival the stories of the other two—but the stories about Pete are totally true. He chose to live as a recluse in the salt marsh that is now known as the Quivira National Wildlife Refuge.

Elias Pelton came from a good family near Medicine Lodge. Selling his share of his father's estate, he came to Stafford County with six horses, a typewriter and $1,500 in his pocket. When the horses eventually died, no one could remember them ever doing any work.

Pete would show up at farmers' homes and eat enormous quantities of food, sometimes going outside and purging himself and then coming back to eat more. Area hunters knew when they came out even for a one-day hunt that they should bring large quantities of food with them. The hunting lodges soon learned to lock up their food stores or when they came back even a week's worth of food would be consumed. His own cooking was mainly wheat shorts, which is used for hog feed, mixed with pork fat and made into pancakes.

Pete could fit a Bible passage into the context of any conversation and quote chapter and verse. He could do advanced mathematic problems in his head as fast as the problem was presented. He could quote Shakespeare and other classic works, and he could always fit them into a conversation.

Above: Pelican Pete in front of the mail-order chicken house. *Courtesy of the Stafford County Historical Museum.*

Right: Pelican Pete at the gate. *Courtesy of the Stafford County Historical Museum.*

Pelican Pete all cleaned up. *Courtesy of the Stafford County Historical Museum.*

Pete took a claim on the salt marsh, and his shack had no floor or roof. When his heat stove would sink until the door would be pushing mud when opened, he would have to jack up the stove. In bad weather, he found it more convenient to stay in bed. Eventually, his shack burned down, and he stayed in a hunting lodge for a while. Then he lived in a shed belonging to the neighboring Meggers family. He saw a prefabricated chicken house in a catalogue and ordered one; he lived in it in the marsh. His ability to show up—just to show up from nowhere—was legendary. Hunters would say they never saw him until the first steak hit the grill.

When Pete wanted or needed to go to town, a neighbor, Fred Meyer, would bring him to his home. He would scrub him, shave him, cut his hair and put him in clean clothes. Meyer kept a general eye on him, dropping by a bag of groceries or other supplies Pete needed from time to time.

At times, when Pete could not take care of himself, he signed himself into the Larned State Hospital. When cleaned up, shaved and dressed, he was a fine-looking man, and friends who would stop for visits would not recognize him. He would winter at the hospital until spring came, and then he would head back to the marsh.

Later in his life, the land he owned was leased for oil at five dollars per acre so the state could get back some of its costs for putting him up. Pete was born on June 1, 1873, in Gracit County, Michigan. It is not known what universities he went to, but it is acknowledged that he was a genius. He was a veteran of the Spanish-American War. He died on May 13, 1945, at Larned State Hospital and is buried in Sharon, Kansas.

Annually, the town of Stafford had a Pelican Pete Pig Out Festival. The festival ran for many years and ended sometime around 2012. Many did not know that Pelican Pete was a real man and not a legend or folklore, but he has moved into the status of legend now.

KRAUSE TORQUE TRACTOR

Many forward-looking inventors and companies have made Kansas a huge incubator for new ideas and advancements. It is not just an individual inventor who has these traits—they have been found in many successful companies that have seen the opportunity to make an advancement or create something new. The advantage of established companies taking up an idea is that resources can be devoted to the idea and the talent that the company has in-house can look to research and development. This can be done and evaluated and not burden the company if it does not make a breakthrough or if it withdraws from the competitive world.

Krause Manufacturing is an example. Starting in Western Kansas in a small farm shop in 1916, Krause built and sold a one-way plow that was especially suited to farming in this arid part of the state. Business grew so fast that a larger and more efficient manufacturing facility was needed. That factory was found in Hutchinson, Kansas, at the defunct Twin Windmill Factory facilities.

With a one-way plow, a farmer could till one hundred acres per day. During World War II, the company was able to get steel allotments because of the need for increased food production. The company also knew that a top-quality product could not be rushed into production.

Krause hired C.J. Carson, who was an engineer in Marshalltown, Iowa, to design a tractor. There were three series of tractors designed. Nothing is known of the first series or if any prototypes were constructed. The first known prototype to be built and tested was in Iowa. It is thought that this tractor is in the collection of Bob Baney, who is also the owner of two tractors that were sent to Colorado for testing on a Krause relative's farm.

The Colorado tractors had been sent out for use on the farm, and the workers were told to "find the weaknesses" of the tractors. The first tractor sent ran on propane and the second on gasoline. They were found to be very powerful, and the one with a PTO was found to run cutters very well. Anytime anything went wrong with the two tractors, they were left for the engineers at the factory to come and repair and investigate the reason for the breakdown. After production plans were dropped by the company, the tractors were left for the use of the farmer, but repair was up to the operator. Since there were no manuals made for the tractors, the prototypes eventually fell into disuse and were parked.

There are no numbers on the total number of prototypes built, but there is a picture of five in the factory. There is an estimate that six to ten could have been built. With five known, it is possible that out there somewhere is a Krause tractor waiting to be found and restored.

The production of Krause tractors was dropped with the advancement of other companies that were established in the tractor business and which were working on new, larger and more powerful models. It is said that the 4010 and its popularity sealed the fate of the Krause tractor being a good investment for the company.

The Krause Company was sold to Kuhn North American, a French company, around 2012. The factory in Hutchinson has been expanded and employs about four hundred workers.

GARLIC SALAD

Even for those who are not surprised at the things in Kansas history that have been dug up and put into this book so far, this may get their attention: garlic salad seems to be a Kansas—and more precisely a Wichita—thing. Food experts, chefs and those who run cooking shows and blog sites all seem to concede that garlic salad is a Wichita thing.

The most famous garlic salad is Doc's from Doc's Steak House on North Broadway in Wichita. When it was announced that Doc's was closing, it sent a shock through the whole region filled with Doc's fans who had eaten at the steakhouse for generations. Go online and you will find many recipes for Doc's particular type of garlic salad. That is because no one had ever been given or purchased the original recipe. The original Doc's has never been duplicated as far as this author has tried to taste. There was a great garlic salad at a BBQ place called Flatland BBQ on West Maple near Friends University. It was good but stronger.

Doc's was not the only steakhouse to offer garlic salad. There was Abe's on Twenty-Ninth Street, Savute's on North Broadway and Ken's Club. The only close approximation that this author has found is at the Nu-way.

The original style of the Wichita garlic salad seems to be southern European. As a customer and avid fan of garlic salad, I have tried to find garlic salad in many locations in and outside of Kansas and have never found one. Although the basic secret of Doc's has been close to being broken, it seems that the key feature was the way that excess moisture was squeezed out of the salad. It was imparted to this author by some in the wholesale food industry that there was a special press that was utilized for this purpose. At this point, this has not been confirmed.

Even with the varied uses of garlic in salads and dressing, the true garlic salad seems to still be a Wichita thing. The obvious style that Doc's salad had was the firmness of the salad, mild flavor and fine texture. Even those who try to duplicate the salad cannot seem to get the texture, dryness or color for which Doc's salad was famous.

HAROLD ENSLEY: THE SPORTSMAN'S FRIEND

Born in Lane County near Healy on a cattle ranch, Harold Ensley fished so much that his mother worried that he would never succeed at anything in life. He was an avid student of history but would skip school to go fishing. Western Kansas would not normally be considered a fisherman's mecca, but Harold spent many hours fishing on Salt Creek. Even with his habit of skipping school, he graduated as valedictorian from the one-room school that the attended.

Harold moved to Joplin, Missouri, where he became a minister in the Church of Christ. He started broadcasting his own Christian radio show. One day, he was trying to sell advertising for his show when a friend commented that he would buy advertisement slots during his radio program if he had a show about fishing. So he started by donating his time for free to create a fishing show. He chose the old Smiley Burnett song "It's My Lazy Day"—which contained the line "Well I might have gone fishin'"—for the show's theme song. Many years later, Smiley would sing the song live on his TV show. The song was rewritten by Nick and Charles Kinny and became "Gone Fishin'."

Harold convinced the local radio station to air *The Fisherman's Friend* show live in 1951. For the first show, it was worrisome if anyone would be listening to it, but the switchboard lit up and they knew they had a hit. By this time, he had moved to Kansas City and was writing a newspaper column. His big break came when Sears sponsored the program five days a week, and that continued for fifteen years.

The Fisherman's Friend became the *The Sportsman's Friend* and ran every week for twenty-one years. When Harold went on TV, his show was one of the first programs to be aired in color. The live show ran for 1,104 telecasts with no reruns. His son, Dusty, filmed all the trips, and they covered everything from snow and water skiing to duck, quail and pheasant hunting, hang gliding and horseback riding in high country, as well as his mainstay, fishing. Extras on the show were his dogs: Ben, an English setter, and Squire, his English pointer. Dusty shot more than 2 million feet of film over the years. Harold's trademark was his red Ford Country Squire station wagon.

In 1975, the show went into syndication and was seen in fifty-four markets in forty-eight states for the next twenty-seven years. The show was produced by the Kansas State Network in Wichita. All total, the show was on the air for forty-eight years. Harold also gained fame by becoming the first world champion for the *Sports Illustrated* fishing tournament the World Series of

Harold Ensley gone fishin' in his red Ford country sedan. *Courtesy of the Kansas State Historical Society.*

Freshwater Sports Fishing. In his life, he went on to receive many awards and honors, including induction into the Broadcasters Hall of Fame, Legends of the Outdoors Hall of Fame and the Kansas Sports Hall of Fame. He also made cameo appearances on TV. He guided Jed Clampett on a fishing trip during an episode of *The Beverly Hillbillies*. He appeared on *Gunsmoke* as one of Festus's drunken cousins who was thrown in jail.

Many celebrities hunted and fished with him over the years, including Ted Williams, Joe DiMaggio, Enos Slaughter, Stan Musial, Bobbie Richardson, Tony Kubek, Roger Maris, George Brett, Mickey Mantle and Roy Rogers. He taught Jimmy Stewart how to cast in a swimming pool and Henry Fonda how to catch trout. He fished with Tennessee Ernie Ford, Karl Malden, Rex Allen, William Holden, Denver Pyle, Mel Tillis, Kirk Douglas, Clint Walker and other notables, including the Apollo 17 astronauts, various governors and senators and a president's son.

Harold's wife, Bonnie, died January 12, 1992, at age seventy. Harold suffered many years with heart problems but never let that slow him down.

He injured his back in a boat accident in Costa Rica. After he ended his show, he wrote two books and was a popular speaker at many events. His last fishing trip was in a wheelchair a few days before he entered a hospital and passed away.

Harold made his home in Overland Park, Kansas. He invented fishing lures, most notably the "Reaper," and marketed merchandise such as his fish coating mix, which was still available as of this writing. He endorsed and had his name on many products, including fishing poles, fillet knives and other items. Harold died on August 24, 2005, at age ninety-two. He was still dreaming of fishing and hunting. He ended every show with the phrase "If you wonder where Harold has gone, just say you saw him in that red Ford Country Sedan and was gone fishin'."

ARKALON AND THE MIGHTY SAMSON

At the crossing of the Cimarron River and what is US 54 Highway today, there is a small roadside park where you can pull off and look at what was one of the engineering marvels of the 1930s. It is still considered a marvel. If you take time to look at the sheer size of the structure and the height of the railroad bed, you will be amazed at what it took to build the bridge at the end of the 1930s. This bridge is the Mighty Samson.

The historical marker placed there will tell the short story of the town of Arkalon and the bridge. The town sprang up because of the river crossing, and the railroad was the reason for that. As with all rivers in the western two-thirds of Kansas, there was a wide floodplain, and bridges were not built for the extreme forces that the periodic flood waters would put on the structures.

The Chicago, Kansas and Nebraska Railroad was built through the area, and the town of Arkalon was created for that purpose. A township was platted around the site, and the town was built. The town was named after the first postmaster's father, Arkalon Tenny. The post office was established in 1888 and remained in operation until 1929. A one-room schoolhouse was built, as were stockyards for shipping cattle to market.

There was one problem with the site: the river itself. Periodically, the railroad bridge would be washed out, and there were several train derailments. By the 1920s, most of the settlers had left town, but the railroad had to keep the train moving, so after every bridge was washed away another one would be quickly built. But the rush job to replace the bridge was soon to be a much more serious problem.

In 1937, the bridge was washed away, and the fast replacement was the site of a major derailment in 1938. The Gold Ball freight train was traveling along the tracks on August 18, 1938. Unbeknownst to the conductor and the crew, the bridge had been washed away in the early morning hours, and the rails were hanging with no support under them. The train crashed into the river below, injuring five men and killing two in the derailment.

The cleanup was soon to become a major attraction as the cars and engine were recovered from the river. So many people gathered to watch the proceedings that hamburger and soda pop stands were set up to take care of the crowds.

The railroad officials had had enough of the constant problems with the bridges over the river. One time the bridge lasted only one month before washing out again. A major engineering and construction effort was soon started with the railroad grade that was 3.5 miles long and raised the tracks to 113 feet above the river below. The massive iron truss bridge is still an architectural wonder to this day. There are 21,800 tons of concrete in the abutments. The length of the Samson is 1,269 feet.

The Mighty Samson Bridge at the townsite of Arkalon, Union Pacific Railroad. *Author's collection.*

The construction of the Mighty Samson Bridge came just in time for World War II. The bridge set a record in 1944 with the highest passenger and freight volume during the war. It also helped produce record revenues for the railroad at the time. The bridge was so important for the war effort that it was guarded during the war. Troops would check the bridge before and after the trains passed over it to prevent sabotage. The bridge is still a vital part of the commerce of the country today. It is considered one of the wonders of Kansas.

Sitting in the roadside park today as the train goes over the bridge is a sight that is a wonder to the rail buff and anyone who appreciates something that was engineered and has lasted so many years since it was built. The Mighty Samson is expected to continue for many more years to come.

BERT WETTA SALES

Alfalfa is a hay crop that grows at a rapid rate. Under ideal conditions, a cutting of the plant can be made about every thirty days. Dry land in Kansas can produce an average of three to four cuttings per season. Under wet conditions or under irrigation, an average of five cuttings can be made. The method of cutting, drying and baling the crop puts it at risk from weather and many other factors that affect quality. Most hay is cut and left to dry before baling. Bale the crop too moist and it can heat up and burn from spontaneous combustion. In the small bale, many farmers have had to salt the layers in the stack to draw moisture from hay that was baled too wet. Several methods of baling hay have been used over the years: small bales, large round, large square and loafs or stacks. Each method has its advantages and disadvantages, but the main goal is quality control.

A banker and businessman from Neodesha was marketing prairie hay and alfalfa hay in the late 1920s and '30s. The man's name was Wright J. Small. In 1930, he was returning by train from Mississippi, where he had purchased a plantation. When he noticed a large steel drum sitting next to the railroad, he got off at the next town and caught a ride back to the location of the drum. There he found a man experimenting with the dehydration process of alfalfa. The hay was brought in fresh cut, dried down, chopped and formed into pellets. The pellets were very well received by growers from chickens to beef. Small made a deal to buy the

Bert Wetta Sales. Alfalfa dehydration plant near Maize. *Courtesy of U.S. Alfalfa.*

process, and it was shipped with an engineer to Neodesha, where the process was perfected.

Joe Wetta grew up in Colwich in the 1930s. He went to Kansas State University and earned a degree in milling sciences. He met Ray Bert while at K State, and they became good friends and fraternity brothers. When the Japanese empire bombed Pearl Harbor, both men joined the service—Joe in the army and Ray in the navy. Both served through the war.

One day in 1946, Joe was standing on a street in Wichita when a familiar voice called out to him. It was Ray. After they caught up on recent years and the war, they began to talk about what they would do from then on. They both talked about the dehydration process. Later that year, the two formed Bert Wetta Sales.

The first dehydration plant was built near Maize along the Missouri Pacific Railroad tracks. They did not know it at the time, but this would soon grow into one of the largest alfalfa milling operations in the middle of America. The company would have plants operating in Larned, Abilene, Mount Hope, Rozel and Stafford, with two plants in Nebraska. They first used pulled field cutters manufactured by Fox. They found that there was a need for something better and self-propelled. This led to the development of the Field Queen Harvester. This self-propelled unit was first built in a shop on Main Street in Maize. As the unit was used and improved, a new business was born.

Field Queen would soon lead the industry in design. Sales soon forced the move to a new plant just west of Maize. But the Field Queen story is another story to be told.

Today, the Bert Wetta Sales Company is known as U.S. Alfalfa, with headquarters in Larned. U.S. Alfalfa is still one of the leading producers of dehydrated feed in the country.

FIELD QUEEN

When Bert Wetta Sales started to process alfalfa with dehydration mills, the harvesting of the alfalfa crop was a long and a frustrating process. The demand for alfalfa pellets was growing, and other companies were getting into the business so competition was becoming fierce. This made efficiency imperative to stay up with the demands of production.

W.J. Small had taken the process and made it practical, and he had a brother named Elmer who designed a pull-type field chopper in the 1940s. This machine would pick up windrowed alfalfa and chop it as it blew it into a truck. This combined processing in the field made operations more efficient at the dehydrator. By 1948, a direct cut head was added so the standing crop could be cut, chopped and blown to be trucked for processing. This gave a better overall control to the quality of the crop as it came in for processing.

In 1947, Bert Wetta started to buy this pull-type unit from the Fox River Tractor Company of Wisconsin. Since the alfalfa fields were scattered over a large area and blowing the crop onto following trucks in the field could create problems in soft fields, a trailer or dolly was built that could be pulled by lighter trucks at less cost.

It was decided to build their own machines since this would give them better ability to improve the machines and add their ideas to the process. The company needed a faster, lighter-weight and more efficient process for harvesting and getting the crop to the plant. They went to a machine shop in downtown Maize that was owned by Vern Van Horn. Ray and Joe were regular customers of the machine shop for parts and machine work. The concept that Joe had for a self-propelled machine was discussed, and in the winter of 1948, machine number one was built. Working from rough drawings, Vern set to work with an employee named Eldon Steen. The first prototype that was self-propelled had two engines. However, the first units used by Bert Wetta were pull-types, which were more likely prototypes of the actual workings of the cutter before making it self-propelled. Three of the pull units were used. Vern was referred to by Ray and Joe as "the genius."

The first self-propelled version of the Field Queen had the drive wheels in the rear, which would be a hallmark for the machine in the future. The name Field Queen was thought to have been coined by Ray's wife. The three pull units were used as a way of refining and improving the first designs. The first self-propelled unit proved that the basic design was sound. The first year, the self-propelled unit cut more than 2,200 tons of processed alfalfa meal.

The first machines were manufactured under the company name Bert-Wetta-Van Horn. In 1948, six units were sold for delivery in the 1949 season to other operators. By August 1949, one large mill had ordered eight Field Queens. The staff was enlarged to six, and the building was expanded. By 1950, the company was in full production. By this time, the machine had become known as the Field Queen Hay Cutter and Field Chopper.

The first manager of the new company was John Prichard, and he brought the company into its first phase. Field Queen was an offshoot to the dehydration business. Most production was done during the winter months, and many farmers were employed. Farmers were great employees since they were mechanically minded, knew how to fix things and were not afraid to suggest or do something different that would improve efficiency.

Vern Van Horn sold his share of the company and retired. He died in 1963 and never had the chance to see the company in its heyday. In 1950, John Prichard was brought in from Stearman Aircraft. He also farmed near Benton. He took part in a major makeover of the factory.

In the 1950s, there was an accident that almost put an end to the new company. A mistake by an employee turned a wrong gas valve on, and gas was vented into the room where John Prichard and a salesman were talking. A cigarette was lit, and an explosion occurred. John was severely burned and escaped the room, but the salesman was killed. John spent months in treatment for multiple burns and injuries.

As time went by, new cutters and changing features were offered. The need for a salesman who could travel between dehydrator plants was apparent, and Joe had a brother named Ben who had been a B-17 pilot in the war. They bought a Cessna Skymaster airplane that Ben would fly and land next to dehydrator plants and take the buying prospect to a facility that was using the Field Queen products for demonstrations.

More and more changes and features were offered, as well as other products. Each buyer had the option of choosing the color for the machines that they ordered. The standard production color would become yellow until the ownership change years later. As far as anyone knows, there are no examples of the first units (from before 1965) that have survived.

In 1966, the Field Queen Cutter had a major makeover due to suggestions by a customer. The new machine was known as the FQC. Units that were equipped with a Detroit Diesel engine were still in use at the Bert Wetta plants at Abilene and Larned. These machines are still operating after forty years.

In 1967, Bernard Wells was hired to run the company. Wells came from Davis Manufacturing. He was given partial ownership opportunities. John Prichard had suffered several heart attacks and assumed a smaller role in the company.

Under Bernard Wells, a new plant was built west of Maize. The downtown facility had been outgrown, and some assembly took place outdoors. With the new plant and expansion, departments were reorganized, and many processes that had been outsourced could be brought back in-house and made more cost-effective.

During this time, Hesston Manufacturing was growing and building swathers and other haying machines. This would be a factor in the Field Queen Company very soon.

Early Field Queen Cutter, front view. *Courtesy of U.S. Alfalfa.*

Field Queen Harvesters cutting alfalfa near Maize, Kansas. *Courtesy of U.S. Alfalfa.*

In 1969, a Field Queen unit was developed that could cut and process silage. This opened the market to farmers as well as dehydration processors. In 1972, even though a dealer network had been set up, larger companies wanted to buy factory direct. This led to the development of a factory sales and service facility.

The original new factory was built with 16,000 square feet of space. Several additions caused the facility to expand to more than 36,550 square feet. In 1972, a major change came to the company with the Hesston Corporation buying property, stock, inventory and all outstanding shares of common stock. The new name was Field Queen, a Division of Hesston Corporation. Field Queen had opened an assembly plant in Coex, France, and this made the company attractive to the growing Hesston Corporation.

The facility grew to 105,000 square feet, and employment reached three hundred. In 1975, a prototype four-wheel-drive tractor was designed and built for Hesston that would have competed against Versatile and Steiger. There was only one built and tested. The tractor was named the Wheel Cat.

This came at a time when Hesston had become deeply mired in financial troubles. Hesston was a corporate conglomerate with eleven divisions. The company sold to Fiat. By 1979, all parts of Field Queen had been closed. All sales and parts had been spun into the Hesston divisions. The last Field Queen unit was sold in 1986. The company eventually dumped all records and manuals of the Field Queen Division. Maize Corporation was started across the road from the old Field Queen plant, and former employees assist owners of Field Queen units with parts and information.

DOROTHY DELAY

Dorothy Delay is regarded as the world's foremost teacher of the violin. She taught some of the greatest violinists of the world: Itzhak Perlman, Cho Liang Lin, Anne Akiko Meyers, Nadja Salerno Sonnenburg, Shlmo Mintz, Nigel Kennedy, Robert McDuffie, Sarah Chang, Mark Kaplan, Rachel Lee, Midori, Gil Shaham and Kyoko Takezawa. Violinists of the Juilliard, Tokyo, Cleveland, American, Takacs, Mendelssohn, Blair, Fine Arts and Vermeer String Quartets studied with her.

Dorothy taught concertmasters of the Berlin Philharmonic, the Philadelphia Orchestra, the Royal Concertgebouw Orchestra of Amsterdam, the Chicago Symphony and many other orchestras the world over. Numerous former students teach at outstanding conservatories in the United States and abroad, including the Aspen Music Festival and School. First prizes were awarded to her students in every major international competition, including the Tchaikovsky, the Queen Elisabeth of Belgium, Montreal, Paganini, Thibaud, Menuhin, Wieniawski, Naumburg, Indianapolis, Queen Sophia of Spain, Chile International, Leventritt, Sarasate, Hanover and Nielson Competitions, among many others.

She was born in Medicine Lodge, Kansas. But in order to appreciate who she was, you have to appreciate who her parents were. Dorothy's grandparents lived on a farm just west of Medicine Lodge. Her parents were Glenn Adney Delay (1882–1955) and Cecile Osborn Delay (1882–1979). At the time Dorothy was born, her parents were at Syracuse, Kansas.

Glenn was the principal and a teacher at Syracuse and was superintendent at Kiowa Kansas Schools, and when Dorothy was in high school, Glenn was principal of Neodesha High School, where Dorothy graduated.

Dorothy spent time with her grandparents near Medicine Lodge, William Osborn and her mother's family were Stoughtons. Both mother and father were educators. Her father was a violinist, and her mother was a violinist and pianist. Her mother is credited for Dorothy's start and progression in music. Dorothy married Edward Newhouse, a writer, but kept her maiden name all her life. Edward described Dorothy as having a "limitless sense of the possible."

When Dorothy was eight years old, she traveled the state with Carrie Nation, the anti-liquor crusader from Medicine Lodge. The girls traveling with Carrie wore angel wings on their backs as they trouped all over the state breaking up bars. Dorothy's father was not happy about that and made sure she was "stripped" of her wings.

Although Dorothy spent her life on the East Coast and traveling the world, her husband commented that "if the East Coast were to break off from the United States and sink into the ocean, she would go right back to the place where she was raised." Through all of her accolades, Dorothy always considered herself to be a Kansan.

At the age of three, Dorothy was reading. She started taking violin lessons at age four and gave her first concert at a local church at age five. In high school, she was found to have an IQ of 180. She was top of her class wherever she was. She entered her senior year of high school at age fourteen. She had to wait a year and a half to enter college. She went to Oberlin at age sixteen, transferring to Michigan State University after a year and graduating at age twenty. She entered Juilliard against her parents' wishes. After graduation, she started to work with the Stuyvesant Trio, which she formed with her sister, who was a gifted cellist.

Dorothy went on to a brilliant career. She conducted seminars all over the world and had a direct impact on the classical music world to this day. Dorothy was born on March 31, 1917, and died on March 24, 2002, in Upper Nyack, Rockland County, New York. She was cremated, and her ashes were given to her husband, who also died in 2002. The location of her ashes is unknown.

FORT SCOTT FOUNDRY AND MACHINE COMPANY: ALBERT W. WALBURN

In the 1890s, Albert W. Walburn was president of the Fort Scott Foundry and Machine Company. Albert—or A.W., as he was known—was born on April 28, 1852, to John and Rachael Walburn. Little is known about his early life, but he ended up in Chicago and went into business.

In the 1870s, he came to Fort Scott and built the foundry and factory for the Fort Scott Foundry and Machine Company. The enterprise was a large employer in the area, and a list of the products that were built there is long and impressive: boilers, brass castings, mining machinery, jail vaults, sheet iron, stoves, building cast-iron fronts, drilling machinery, horse powers, iron railings, coal trucks, grates, portable and stationary engines, pulleys, shafts, rock crushers, rock breakers, evaporation systems, sugar processors, steam engines, windmills, sawmills, ore treatment machinery, farm equipment, household equipment, concentrators, smelters, steam and water pipes, glue evaporators, gelatin evaporators, tank water extractors, pepsin extractors and much more.

The company would design and ship an entire processing center for sugar making or mining refining. The company shipped systems and equipment to places like the Sandwich Islands, Texas, Oklahoma, Utah, Cuba, South America and any place that had need of producing a product by steam or crushing.

Meatpacking companies such as Armour and Swift would use huge evaporators made by the company. A.W. worked closely with Mr. M. Swenson, who had patented the Swenson method of evaporators and was a very prolific inventor of processes and machinery. Swenson bought a half interest in the Fort Scott foundry, and the name was changed to the Walburn-Swenson Foundry and Machine Company. A.W. was very forward-thinking and built an electrical company for Fort Scott that later became the municipally owned utility. He was also on the board of directors of the St. Louis, Fort Scott and Wichita Railroad. The company cast and made parts for locomotives and railcars.

A.W. made the society pages when he married Mary Virginia Gentry in a double wedding ceremony with her sister, Nannie, who married William R. Estill. The ceremony took place in her home town of Sedalia, Missouri. A.W. and his wife resided in Fort Scott.

It can be assumed that the attraction of the foundry to the area was the proximity of the coal and other mining fields in southeastern Kansas, including lead, zinc and other minerals. The area also attracted a large group of immigrants that provided a skilled labor pool for mining and manufacturing. The location in the central part of the country and access to rail shipping also helped. However, there was a point reached when even these advantages were not enough to keep the company located in Kansas. With the international business it was doing, the increased volume soon outgrew the capacity of the region. The major business centers were also in Chicago and New York. It had to be a shock when the announcement was made to move all the machinery to a new plant in Chicago Heights and offices to New York.

In 1900, A.W. retired from active business after selling the company, which then was renamed the American Foundry and Machinery Company. A.W. moved to an estate in the Knollwood Park addition of Elmsford, New York, and named his estate The Little House. He was a neighbor of John D. Rockefeller, who was a frequent golfing buddy, and they became good friends. A.W. was also an avid amateur photographer with twenty-five images in the Kansas State Historical Society's collection. He died in 1930.

Mr. Swenson, being independent after the sale of the company, invented a hydraulic method of extracting salt and evaporating it.

FRANKFORT: ULTIMATE SACRIFICE

Willard Backman was a member of the B-17 bomber "In the Mood" crew. The bomber went down in the North Atlantic, and the bodies were never recovered. This sad story of sacrifice is something that most communities in the country had to deal with, as their young people went to serve in the nation's service. But Frankfort in Marshall County probably has had the most sacrifice to deal with and the distinction of having the highest per capita loss of servicemen in World War II.

The town of Frankfort was laid out in 1867 when the Central Branch of the Union Pacific Railroad was built. The town was named for Frank Schmidt, who was a member of the town company. The town was incorporated in 1875. The town sits on the Oregon Trail, and the historical marker there will tell you about Alcove Springs and the Oregon Trail and how it was a favorite stopping spot for those heading west.

The town is a very attractive place, and there are many buildings and homes that have been restored. The town shows its pride. It is the pride of loss that is found on a highway sign dedicated to the Frankfort servicemen who made the ultimate sacrifice. To understand the impact that the war had on a community, just imagine the number when applied to your hometown—what kind of impact would it have and the effect that would last through the generations.

On November 16, 2006, Senator Pat Roberts read into the *Congressional Record* the names of thirty-two men who did not come back from the war. According to Senator Roberts, "What makes this town notable is the solemn fact that thirty-two men from Frankfort and the surrounding farmland gave their lives in World War II." He continued: "Based on the records from the local county newspapers of that time, it is concluded that the Frankfort community lost more men in World War II than any town of similar size."

Roberts credited Topekan Frank Benteman, an army veteran of World War II, with sharing the story. Benteman's wife had bought five scrapbooks at an auction for one dollar each. The story of the losses to the Frankfort community came from the old newspaper clippings in the scrapbooks. The woman who had compiled the scrapbooks had two brothers who had served in the war.

The bill to honor the lost servicemen was approved by legislation in 2012, and the dedication took place on Highway K-99 on June 16. It was not the only sacrifice that the town had made. Six men were lost in World War I as well. In total, Marshall County lost ninety-six men in World War II. A plaque with the county's servicemen's names is at Main and Sixth in Blue Rapids.

The names of Frankfort's fallen are as follows: Willard A. Backman, Fred Bentsen, Lloyd C. Blackney, Leland Cook, Dale C. Cooper, Melvin Cope, Elmer Crumpton, Kenneth Dewalt, Robert Emmingham, Victor Feldhausen, Peter Fiegenr, William R. Gibson, Don Hockensmith Jr., Milan E. Jester, Koester Johnson, Donald E. King, Vern F. Long, Weldon Maneval, Matt McKean, Carl O. Nord, Aloysius Noud, Munro Oellner, Howard Olson, Charles Poff, Paul A. Puden, Charles L. Puteney, Theodore Rhodes, David L. Shyne, James Stoffel, Clifford Watson, Robert B. Welsh and Charles F. Zinn.

The war has passed from the generations, and not many are left at this writing who went through the horror and sacrifice that this generation did. It is too easily forgotten why these men made the sacrifice that they were called to give. It is hoped that the legacy of these men's lives serves as a reminder that the cost of freedom is not cheap, and as time goes on, each generation must renew the sacrifice and remember why these men are not here except in memory.

GILBERT TWIGG: MASS MURDERER

One of the dark "firsts" that occurred in Kansas has largely been forgotten. On August 13, 1903, thirty-year-old Gilbert Twigg committed what is considered the first mass murder of modern times in Winfield, Kansas. It is a sad chapter and a long, convoluted story that may go back to his family origins. Twigg came from a prominent family from western Maryland; the Twiggs were a large family and were basically divided into two groups. One side was called the "Blue Eyed Twiggs" and the other the "Brown Eyed Twiggs." Although prolific and prominent, they were at times at odds with each other, even to the point of violence.

Gilbert was a member of the Blue Eyed Twiggs and followed an uncle to Winfield. There he found work at Burden at a flour mill. He seemed a normal lad and eventually was engaged to a local lady of good family. For some unknown reason, the marriage was broken off by the lady, and a long period followed that seemed to set Twigg on his doomed path.

Twigg joined the army cavalry and was hoping for deployment to Cuba, but the unit was passed over. Wanting to see combat, he transferred to the Signal Corps and went to Cuba for the duration of the Spanish-American War. He did not see combat during his deployment, and after his enlistment and discharge were over, he was listed as mustering out in New York. He then reenlisted for another three-year tour. He went to the Philippines during the bloody insurrection that followed the Spanish-American War. By the time of his discharge, he had made sergeant and had a clean service record, but some think there was something that was not listed on his record.

Twigg went to Great Falls, Montana, where he worked in a flour mill. He wrote a friend a letter telling how he enjoyed his work and loved Montana, but for some reason, he eventually returned to Winfield. In Winfield and the surrounding communities, he applied for jobs, especially in the flour milling industry, but even his old employer did not hire him. Kids and people around town came to call him "Crazy Twiggs." His long-lost love had married and moved to Wichita and was raising a family. Twigg hung around Winfield, spending a lot of time in the parks. Apparently, he was nursing grudges against many people, real and imagined. One day, he went to the hardware store and bought a twelve-gauge shotgun and a variety of ammunition. The owner thought the choice of ammo was a little odd and asked what he was planning on shooting with it? He replied, "I don't know yet." As an afterthought, he bought a .32-caliber handgun. During the week, he bought more shotgun shells at different stores.

On August 13, 1903, Winfield was enjoying one of its favorite pastimes, a band concert. The town was busy, and there was a large crowd. Twigg, dressed in a khaki buckskin coat and dark pants, visited his uncle. His uncle thought him a bit strange but did not inquire about his attire and the fact that he was carrying a shotgun. He assumed that he had been hunting. Twigg crept up an alley, although witnesses thought he acted confident. He was an accomplished marksman and took a kneeling position as he had been taught in the army. A boy saw him and was told to leave because Twigg did not want to hurt him, that he was going to do some "tall shooting." Twigg looked at the bandstand and muttered, "I wonder if I can get Camen?" Camen was the band leader. He started shooting, hitting a horn player and his instrument and another man. It was after the second shot that Camen noticed what was going on.

It is estimated that the random shooting only took five to eight minutes. In all, nine people would die, and up to thirty were wounded. At the end, as officers and others were rushing him, he pulled the pistol as he fell on a pile of iron he was using, putting a bullet in his head. Immediate reports were that he had committed suicide. Another version, believed by many, was that he was shot by a local night patrolman for the police department and a popular member of the community with his rifle and a .45 pistol. Since Twigg had shot himself after going down, it is more likely that Officer George Nichols actually took him down. Officer Nichols did not take credit for taking Twigg down, and the coroner's jury did not investigate all the circumstances. Nichols was the first and only black officer in Winfield. Although there is no record of racial problems in Winfield, it was thought best left alone that a black officer had shot a white man.

Although there have been many other mass murders since, this random act of violence is considered the first of its kind in psychiatric and criminal circles.

GUNNY

If you are in the Marine Corps and hear that name, you know what it stands for: gunnery sergeant. If you are a movie buff or watch television or even see a commercial and hear "Gunny," you are looking at a Kansas boy. Born near Emporia, Gunny's family moved near Kansas City, where he lived until he was fourteen years old. In an interview, he said, "You know how you think that when you are a success you will come home and buy the family farm? Well I came home to buy the farm and it was a parking lot! They built the Kansas Speedway on our old farm and they would not sell it back to me."

If you still don't know who this is, it is about R. Lee Ermey. When his family moved to the state of Washington, he was getting into trouble. A judge looked down and said, "This is the second time I have seen you, we will need to do something about it." The judge asked if he liked sunshine; he said he did and was given the choice of going into the service or to "where the sun doesn't shine." He said he liked sunshine. His dad had been in the navy, so he went there, and it did not want him because of his troubles. He stumbled into a Marine Corps recruiting office, and the sergeant jumped up and said, "You are a farm boy, aren't you?" He wanted to know how many pull-ups he could do, so he did ten right there. The recruiter told him, "The Marines want you." Boot camp wasn't much different than living at home with all his brothers and a dad that had to ride herd on all of them. Ermey spent eleven years in the Marine Corps and retired with an injury. He spent fourteen months in Vietnam and two tours in Okinawa. He spent two years as drill instructor in India Company, Third Recruit Training Battalion, at MCRD San Diego, retiring with the rank of staff sergeant. He was promoted post-service to gunnery sergeant, the only one to be promoted this way, due in large part to his exemplary portrayal of the Marine ethic in film as a Marine Corps ambassador and patriot.

Gunny's work as an actor has made him immediately recognizable, and his roles are too numerous to count here. But one highlight is playing Sergeant Hartman in Stanley Kubrick's *Full Metal Jacket*. On that movie, Gunny was hired on as technical adviser. Kubrick fired the original actor and cast Gunny, allowing him to rewrite half the part. For this Gunny was awarded the Boston Society of Film Critics award for Best Supporting Actor of 1987 and earned a Golden Globe nomination.

He had other roles in *Apocalypse Now, Dead Man, Switchback*, remakes of *Willard* and *Texas Chainsaw Massacre*, as well as the prequel, *Texas Chainsaw Massacre: The Beginning*, and all three *Toy Story* movies. He was also in *Mississippi Burning, Purple Hearts, The Siege of Firebase Gloria, Dead Man Walking, Se7en, Fletch Lives* and *Leaving Las Vegas*. He lent his voice to several projects like *The Simpsons, Family Guy, SpongeBob SquarePants* and others. He often had up to fifteen new scripts at a time he was reviewing for new parts and said that he had to fight for free time. He brought a sense of reality to every part he played.

Gunny hosted documentary series *Mail Call* and *Lock n' Load with R. Lee Ermey*. He was in many commercials and was removed from one company's commercials because of his outspokenness for the military and critiquing President Obama with his attitude toward the troops. The owner of the company was a close friend of President Obama's. He also had a show running at this time called *Gunny Time*.

Gunny was a staunch supporter of the military. He conducted morale tours visiting U.S. troops in locations such as Al Kut, Iraq and Bagram Airfield, Afghanistan. He held a USO show in which he portrayed Gunnery Sergeant Hartman and conducted comedy routines, and he did the same at Doha, Qatar and Kuwait City in 2003.

In case you didn't think that Gunny was the real deal, check out his ribbons: Combat Action Ribbon, Meritorious Unit Commendation, Good Conduct Medal with two 3/16" Bronze Stars, National Defense Service Medal, Armed Forces Expeditionary Force Medal, Vietnam Service Medal with one 3/16" Silver Star, Marine Corps Drill Instructor Ribbon, Republic of Vietnam Gallantry Cross with Palm, Republic of Vietnam Campaign Medal, Rifle Marksmanship and Pistol Sharpshooter.

Gunny sadly passed away on April 15, 2018. He was laid to rest at Arlington National Cemetery, Branch U.S. Marine Corps, Section 83, Grave 54, on January 18, 2019. In Gunny's honor, the City of Palmdale, California, renamed North Avenue as R. Lee Gunny Avenue. Gunny lived in Palmdale the last twenty years of his life.

IRA D. BROUGHER: BARTON COUNTY

Born in York County, Pennsylvania, Ira Brougher was one of nine children of Samuel and Lydia Brougher. Born on May 14, 1943, he died on May 17, 1920, and is buried at Great Bend Cemetery. He was an industrious homesteader who helped organize the South Bend Township in Barton County and served as its first trustee. Being oriented to public service, he became Barton County clerk in 1877. He served as clerk of the district court in 1889 during the term of Judge Clark. Brougher also helped form the Barton County Fair Association and served as president. He was also a director of the German-American Bank.

As an industrious farmer, he developed his land and ended up owning nine quarter-sections of land: seven in Barton County, one in Stafford County and one in Hodgeman County. Working cooperatively with his neighbor Frank Dell, his farm was described as one of the finest in the area. What makes this out of the ordinary is that he had lost his right arm in the Civil War, and his neighbor was minus one leg.

Ira enlisted in the 130th Regiment Pennsylvania Volunteer Infantry, Company F. He lost his right arm at the Battle of Antietam. He was discharged and later enlisted in the Railroad Corps. For some reason, not reported, he was present at the Battle of Gettysburg. The story from the *Kansas City Gazette* from June 1915 described Ira's actions at Gettysburg: "[He provided] himself a repeating revolver and plunged into the thickest of the fighting of this great battle though he was no longer in the service."

Listening to the admonition "Go west, young man, go west," he came directly to Barton County, Kansas. He proved to be an intrepid businessman and public servant. He commissioned a bronze statue to honor Civil War soldiers from Chicago. It is a one-of-a-kind bronze casting called *The Rifleman*. It has stood near the Barton County Courthouse for one hundred years. Most memorial statues of the time were ordered from catalogues and were of standard sizes and subjects. This statue is unique, and after a long time, it started showing its age. Ron Harvey was commissioned to restore and repair the statue, and it was the subject of public celebration in November 2015.

JESSE HARPER: KANSAS RANCHER WHO HIRED KNUTE ROCKNE

Jessie Claire Harper was an American football and baseball player, coach, athletic director and rancher. Born in East Paw, Illinois, he was inducted into the College Hall of Fame in 1971. I will not go into his record as a coach because this story is about the Kansas connection to both the University of Notre Dame and to Knute Rockne.

Notre Dame had ten football coaches from 1889 to 1912. The school had been ostracized by the Western Conference (Big 10) because of the school being Catholic. The "Fighting Irish" name, along with the mascot, came a long time afterward. Early on, the team was simply known as "The Catholics." A commitment was made to the athletic department, which had been losing money every year. It hired twenty-nine-year-old Jesse Harper

Left: Notre Dame coach, athletic director and Kansas rancher Jesse Harper, near Sitka. *Courtesy of the University of Notre Dame Archives.*

Below: The coaches. *Left to right*: Ewald O. Steihm (University of Nebraska), Knute Rockne and Jesse Harper. *Courtesy of the University of Notre Dame Archives.*

to serve as athletic director, head football coach, head basketball coach and baseball coach from 1913 through 1917.

Harper would create a legacy that affects the school to this day and proved to be an innovator of the passing attack. After persuading Army to play Notre Dame, he awed the eastern press and put Notre Dame on the map. Harper had hired Knute Rockne to be an assistant after recommending him to the University of Kansas. He almost lost Rockne when Michigan State offered him its head football coach position. Harper convinced Rockne to stay, promising that Rockne would succeed him.

Harper stepped down and came to Kansas, where his father owned a twenty-thousand-acre cattle ranch near Sitka in Clark County. Harper's father was in the cattle business and had moved to Iowa and then to Kansas. While managing the ranch, Harper lived in Wichita and commuted to Sitka to conduct business.

Harper remained friends with Knute Rockne, and they visited quite often when Rockne flew through Wichita. Rockne also had a friendship with KU's Phog Allen. Rockne also consulted with Charlie Bachman of Kansas State University football on strategy to beat Nebraska. Another Kansas tie for Rockne was when Notre Dame almost played Haskell Indian Institute in the Rose Bowl.

When Rockne's airplane crashed near Matfield Green, Harper drove up to identify the body and escorted the body home. On the spot, Notre Dame rehired Harper to run the athletic program. The school had built a fifty-thousand-seat stadium but had an average eighteen thousand attendance.

Depression hit the ranch, and it was mortgaged for more than it was worth and went into foreclosure. Harper's salary allowed him to buy the ranch back for fifty cents on the dollar. He returned home to the ranch, where he raised a son who became a college football player and a coach—but not at Notre Dame.

Jesse Harper was born on December 10, 1883, in DeKalb County, Illinois, and died on July 31, 1961, in Sitka, Kansas.

B-29 TRAGEDY AT COPELAND

The town of Copeland is in an area of vast fields of wheat, corn and grass. Farming and ranching is the major industry of the area. The railroad played a major role in the location and development of the town. The town was like dozens of others in the state where people lived, worked, worshiped and played. It is the site of the first wind farm in Kansas. During World War II, it was the site of a terrible crash of a B-29 bomber. The circumstances made the tragedy even more terrible to the community as the pilot had connections to the community and was well liked. The story of the B-29 crash is printed in Ward's *History of Early Day Copeland, Kansas.*

On a Sunday night, a half mile south of Copeland, a B-29 Super Fortress crashed into the home of O.H. Hatfield. In the home were Mr. Hatfield and his grandson Jay Dean Settles. Both were killed in the crash and resulting fire. In the home at the time were also Mrs. Hatfield and their daughter, Mrs. Dean Settles. Both were blown through the wall into the yard, seriously injured. Neighbors found the two women walking around the yard with burns, bruises and lacerations. The two women were loaded into a car and taken to St. Anthony's Hospital in Dodge City.

The full story of the circumstances may never be known, but at 9:30 p.m., the plane flew low over Copeland. The bomber was stationed at Walker Airfield at Hays. They identified the copilot as Lieutenant Lawrence Eslinger. Lieutenant Eslinger was the nephew of Copeland residents Mrs. V.E. Reese and Sam and Sterling Somerville. He was the son of Mr. and Mrs. Harold Eslinger of Manhattan, Kansas. The family had resided for many years at Kinsley, and Lawrence spent many summers in the Copeland area, working summers during high school and college on farms in the community. He had been an active part of the community and church life of Copeland.

The father of Jay Dean Settles, the baby who was killed, was Captain Dean Settles, who had just been on furlough following thirty-five successful missions over German-held territory in a B-17 Flying Fortress. His wife had just returned home from the East Coast, where she had accompanied him as he reported for another overseas tour.

Reverend M.R. Hines had just read a passage to the Sunday evening congregation when the sound of distressed motors drowned out his voice. The landing lights lit up the countryside as the bomber came down, touching its wing tip on the ground just south of town. The plane left a trail of debris for a half mile and flipped into the farm home and buildings of the Hatfield farm. High-octane fuel spilled over the area, and a huge fire ensued. There were outbuildings that held nine thousand bushels of wheat that all went up in flames. There was also three hundred gallons of gasoline in a tank that added to the fire. The scene was described as a literal holocaust. Added to the fire were explosions from seven dummy bombs that were loaded with four pounds of black power. All of these exploded, and one was found in the cellar under the farmhouse. Two of the engines were found more than a half mile west of the crash scene.

Ten crew members on the B-29 died in the crash. With the two on the ground, twelve lives total were lost. Lieutenant Eslinger had a clear tenor voice and had sung with a local quartet. Mr. Hatfield was a builder of the community and had constructed all the buildings on the farm. As of the writing of the history in 1960, there were many structures still standing that he had built.

Compounding the tragedy was that the plane and crew were ready to ship out to the South Pacific and this was one of the last training lights. Blame was placed on Second Lieutenant W.B. Cooper, who was piloting the aircraft. It had been reported that the aircraft had flown low over the community before.

This event brought home directly to the members of the community the horrors of war and sacrifices that were made by a nation.

BAILOR PLOW MANUFACTURING COMPANY

Kansas was fertile ground for the invention and manufacturing of farm equipment. Atchison had a thriving company that boosted the local economy for several years. It came in the name of Silas Edward Bailor and the Bailor Plow Manufacturing Company. Bailor was born in Warren County, Ohio, on Christmas Day 1857. His family moved in 1876 to Nebraska, where he attended public school and graduated from Geneva High School. He married Della Adams and began farming five miles south of Geneva.

While farming, Bailor also worked at a foundry in Geneva, and he designed and built the first successful two-row cultivator in 1892. He then sold the patent to the Dempster Manufacturing Company of Beatrice, Nebraska. His cultivator won "Highest Award" at the 1904 Louisiana Purchase Exposition in St. Louis.

The Atchison Commercial Club was looking for a profitable business to add to the local economy. In 1912, Bailor and friends started the Bailor Cultivator Company. He produced cultivators, listers, harrows and other machines. Many of the machines and implements were used throughout the lighter-soil Corn Belt.

The company built a motor-driven cultivator that was of a three high wheel design that resembled the row crop tractors that would come later.

The thought was to wean farmers off horse power; the lightweight design of the motor cultivator was easier to handle and control than the huge traction machines that were being produced at that time. The drawback of the machine was the cost ($500) and the fact that it was used such a short time during the season.

The relocation and creation of the company in Atchison started well, with the sale of one hundred of the new motor cultivators. By 1915, Bailor had sold $250,000 worth of machinery from the twenty-five-thousand-square-foot facility at 1302 North Main. The firm had forty employees and had a payroll of $50,000 per year. The machine was sold and listed by the Oliver Chilled Plow Company in its 1914 catalogue. By 1925, it was not listed anymore.

The Bailor Plow Company made a large variety of specialty wrenches that were designed to be used with the company's machines and implements. Today, Bailor wrenches are highly collectable and sought after.

The 1919 motor cultivator had a four-cylinder Leroi engine. There was a smaller version made that was powered by a Cushman engine. A Blackhawk corn or bean planter was available to extend the usefulness of the machine. The total number of motor cultivators built is unknown. In the 1920s, Bailor sold his interest in the company. The federal census listed him at Washita, Oklahoma, in 1920 and 1930.

Sometime around 2010, the Bailor family Bible was found in Kent County, Texas. With family history and several photographs, it is not known how the Bible found its way to Texas. Silas Bailor died in 1948 in Wellington, Kansas, at the age of ninety-one.

The Bailor Company was listed in catalogues until the 1930s. It is easy to assume that the company was one of the victims of the Depression and Dust Bowl.

BAUGHMAN FARMS

This story starts with Henry Clay Baughman, who was born in Stringtown, Muskingum County, Ohio. He married his wife, Rosannah, on March 20, 1866, in Stovertown, Ohio. During the Civil War, he was captain of Company F, Fifty-Ninth Illinois Infantry. After their marriage, they resided in Thomasboro, Champaign County, Illinois, where they had five children. Sometime between 1875 and 1879, the family moved to Reno County,

Kansas. Henry and Rosannah lived the last years of their life in Cheney and are buried at the Pioneer Cemetery just north of town. At one point, Henry served as mayor.

Henry's son, John William, moved to Morton County, where he started to farm. When he first arrived, he worked with surveyors and became interested in farm ground. As he figured out how to farm and flourish in that arid area of the state, he accumulated more and more land. He would accumulate so much land in Kansas and Colorado that he acted as a real estate agent for his own properties. He would advertise in papers over a large region offering properties for sale.

The southwest part of Kansas is not an easy place to farm, and many would become discouraged and give up or just plain go broke. John would put tenants on his farms, and the successful ones he would encourage to purchase the property. He accumulated more and more property, and as of 1916, he had accumulated 31,868 acres of land. In the process, he expanded into oil, cattle and feedlots. By the time John died in 1954, he had accumulated 300,000 acres of land in Kansas and Colorado, making him one of the biggest landowners in the country.

John and his wife, Ella (née Williamson) had one son, Robert, born in 1907. Together, father and son expanded their holdings and business. Both had a huge interest in history and accumulated collections that now reside with the Kansas State Historical Society in Topeka. Both men authored several books about Kansas. Robert is well known for the books *Kansas in Maps*, *Kansas in Newspapers* and *Early Day Post Offices*.

John died in 1954 and Robert died in 1970. After Robert's death, the huge landholdings were sold to Kansas-born billionaire Phillip Anschutz. A large part of the estate was put into the Baughman Foundation, which gives more than $1 million per year to causes and students in a three-state area.

John and Robert had a major impact on southwest Kansas and southeastern Colorado. Many of the families who worked the farms as tenants, as long as three generations, were encouraged to become landowners. There are a lot of families who farm today who owe their beginnings to the Baughmans.

BLUE VALLEY MANUFACTURING AND FOUNDRY

Fredrick A. Marlatt was a farmer and an assistant professor of entomology at Kansas State Agricultural College. In 1897, he quit the college to concentrate on his farming and the businesses he had purchased. Blue Valley Manufacturing and Foundry in Manhattan produced many items for the farm, including windmills, Little Wonder butter churns, feed mills, grinding mills, corn harvesters, stove grates, sash weights, aluminum and bronze castings and cultivators.

The business was located at 706 North Fourth Street in Manhattan. By the 1920s, the business employed one machinist, one foundry man and a dozen more workers when castings were being poured. Part of the truck scale can still be seen next to the curb. There was a separate carpenter's shop where the pattern shop was located. The company also did general foundry work and repairs of all kinds.

Marlatt was very busy with community affairs, being a member of the Methodist Episcopal Church and the Epworth League and was active in the Republican Party and many other community affairs. He married Annie E. Lindsey, who was an instructor in domestic science at the Kansas State Agriculture College, on August 20, 1913. Fredrick's sister, Abby Lillian Marlatt, who graduated from KSAC, became an educator starting in Utah and then in Rhode Island, and then she became the first director of the Home Economics Department at the University of Wisconsin.

The Marlatt family was very prominent in the area, beginning with Fredrick's father, Washington, who was one of the original settlers in the area. He bought his Bluemont Farm from a man named Jim Wilson, who was hired to survey the town of Manhattan. Wilson had come upriver, and the steamboat he came on was grounded at the site for some time.

Washington Marlatt's home is in the National Register of Historic Places and is owned by Kansas State University. The home was used for many years as the residence for dairy workers at the college. Parts of the materials from the original barn were used in the construction of one of the dairy barns at KSU. The Washington Marlatt home is located at 1600 College Avenue.

There is a Marlatt Park on the campus of Kansas State University, and there is a Marlatt Street in Manhattan. There is also a stone wall from the Marlatt farm that has been studied as an archaeological site and recorded by the university.

LONE TREE MASSACRE, 1874

The "Lone Tree" was a well-known landmark on the east side of Crooked Creek. This was about forty miles south and twenty miles west of Dodge City, or six miles southeast of Meade. A survey party that was laying out townships was working on the exterior lines of Township 33. The group was to be away from base camp for a week. Captain Short was in charge of this team, which included his son, Daniel Truman Short, age fourteen; James Shaw, age fifty-one, and his son, J. Allen Shaw, age eighteen; Harry C. Jones, age twenty-two; and John H. Keuchler, age seventeen.

The group was working under a contract from the surveyor general of Kansas, Carmi W. Babcock. These men were mostly from Douglas County and were students of the University of Kansas. This group was part of a larger group working on surveying and platting southwest Kansas at the time.

Two different parties went out in different directions to do the work, and a member of the other party saw Captain Short's wagon standing on the east side of Crooked Creek about eight and a half miles south and two and a half miles west of Meade. He notified the leader of the other team, Captain Thrasher, and reconnoitered with his force. There he found the bodies of Captain Short and his five men lying on the ground in a row as they had been left by the Indians. The oxen were dead in their yokes, with their hind quarters cut off, and the camp dog lay dead beside his master. Captain Short, his son and Harry Jones had been scalped and the others' heads crushed. The pockets of all had been turned inside out. There were twenty-eight bullet holes in the wagon, and eight bullet holes were found in the water barrel.

James Shaw was the last man killed, as shown by the tracks made by the irons on his boot heels. Later, it was learned that they had carried off their own dead and wounded. After a careful search, the bodies were put in Short's wagon and brought back to camp. They were buried there at sundown about one hundred yards east of the Lone Tree. One grave three feet deep was made for all the men to be buried in. They were wrapped in tent cloth. Initials were carved into stones and placed at the head of each body.

The signs of the fight showed that it had been a running battle from the wagon. They tossed out the water barrel, the mess kit and other equipment to make room for the bodies of those killed in the fight. The fight was evident for three and a half miles, leaving a trail of cartridge cases and equipment, and showed that it was a desperate battle.

Later on, it was found that the Cheyenne woman warrior Mochi (Buffalo Calf) had been part of the band. Mochi had been a member of Black Kettle's band and witnessed her mother shot in the head at the Sand Creek Massacre. The soldier who entered the tent and shot her mother had tried to rape her, and she shot him with her grandfather's rifle. She had escaped the camp with other survivors and evaded Chivington's men, who tried to kill all of the Indians in the camp. She became a warrior and fought alongside her husband for eleven years; she was the only woman to be incarcerated by the United States Army as a prisoner of war. The group was from Chief Medicine Water's band.

Truman Short's horse was later found in Medicine Water's camp about one hundred miles west of Camp Supply. The raiding party consisted of twenty-five warriors. The army dispatched three hundred soldiers to bring the Cheyennes back to the reservation. That group had passed by Short's camp. When the soldiers had passed the surveyors earlier, it was asked that a small detachment be left behind to protect the surveyors, but the officer said he had no authority to do so and noted that there were no Indians in the area.

Mrs. Short was still in charge of her husband's contract to complete the survey, and she commissioned Captain Thrasher of Dodge City to finish the contract in addition to his own. Mrs. Short determined that the bodies of the surveyors should be removed at the same time from near Lone Tree and moved to a permanent burial place. She was aided in this by the surveyor general of Kansas and General John Pope of Fort Leavenworth.

WHAT KANSAS'S SHAPE COULD HAVE BEEN

Find any border map of the state, and you will see a line on the ground that marks the end (or start) of Kansas. On most roads near the border, there will be a sign that tells you that you are now in Kansas. How did it get that way? Why are there two Kansas Citys? Well the Kansas-Nebraska Act—and the historic struggles associated with it—is pretty well known, but how did the final shape of Kansas become Kansas? Politics.

This is, of course, simplistic, but the story is made up of many parts and circumstances. The original western boundary of the state was the Continental Divide. This is why the area of Cherry Creek and the mountains was called the "Kansas Gold Fields." At the establishment of Colorado, the Kansas legislature felt that the eastern part of the state did not want anything to do with governing the mining areas. The territory was considered to be too long for a state. The area between Western Kansas and Eastern Colorado contained nothing of value, and everything west of what is now US 281 was almost put in Colorado. It was believed that the area had more in common with Denver than Topeka (some still believe that).

A booklet named *Boundary Lines of Kansas* included speeches made to the Old Settlers Association at Alma on September 28, at Independence on October 16 and at the Banquet at Kansas City on October 18, 1909, by George W. Martin, the secretary of the Kansas State Historical Society.

Without repeating the entire booklet and circumstances, suffice it to say the shape of Kansas could have been much different. The Kansas-Nebraska Act set the southern boundary of Nebraska (and the northern boundary of Kansas) along the 40th parallel, west to British America. The southern boundary ran west about thirty miles north of the southwest corner of Missouri to the border of the New Mexico Territory. The eastern boundary ran from the southeast corner north to Kansas City to the middle of the river, where the Republican River joined the Missouri River. The western boundary was originally the Continental Divide. The

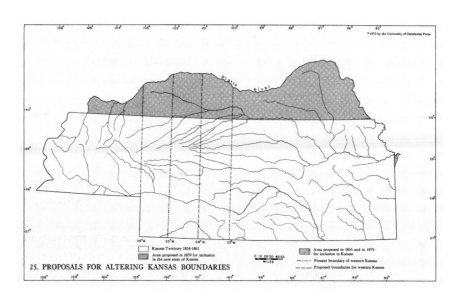

A map of what Kansas could have looked like. *From* Historic Maps of Kansas *(Oklahoma Press, Socolofsky and Self, 2nd edition).*

boundary was completed by following the Missouri River, cutting off the northeast corner of the state.

There was a movement and a petition sent to Congress from Kansas City, Missouri, wanting to join as one town with Kansas City, Kansas. The carrier of that petition was distracted by a young lady and went to Europe for two years, so the petition never progressed further. The *Kansas City Times* published what would have been a revised map of Kansas by squaring off Kansas and the five counties in Missouri that would have been a part of Kansas. There was popular support for the changes on all sides, but it was not to be. The combination of two processes, one in the 1850s and the other in the 1870s, left the boundaries as we know them today.

There was another change proposed in the border of Kansas and Nebraska. The Platte River was a formidable river to cross, and bridge technology was not highly advanced at the time. The people on the south side of the Platte were effectively cut off from the other part of the territory and then state. The settlers petitioned for everything south of the Platte River to be joined to Kansas. The Kansas legislature took up the petition, and it would have been accepted but for one thing: Kansas was mostly Republican, and the area south of the Platte was Democratic. There was a fear of the Democrats gaining a majority in the legislature, so it was turned down.

The many opportunities to change the shape of the state were halted due to a variety of reasons, with politics being the biggest. Due to continued beliefs from Topeka that the area west of US 281 to the Colorado border echo original attitudes, there is periodically a movement to divide the state and create a formal Western Kansas. So far, there has been no popular vote sufficient for this movement to progress.

It is safe to say that Colorado is happy with the final boundaries, and bridges took care of the problems for Nebraska. The disputes over the Cherokee Strip and the boundaries of Indian Territory are a whole different story.

KANSAS WILDLIFE LAW ENFORCEMENT

At the time J.R. Mead penned his book *Hunting and Trading on the Great Plains, 1859–1875*, he had first settled on the Smoky Hill River not far from what is now Salina. He described the buffalo herds that numbered in the millions and the numbers of elks, birds, wolves, bears, cougars and many other species that thrived on the vast grasslands. He described the rivers in the area as clear and cold, but they remained so for only fifteen years after the plow came to turn under the sod and grow crops.

At the time that Mead came and worked as a hunter and trader, the abundance of wildlife was surely thought inexhaustible. But of course, that changed; that the last kill of buffalo near Wichita, which Mead helped found, was around 1873 at the Cowskin Creek Crossing. The location would be known as Griffenstien's Crossing and today is Twenty-First Street and the Cowskin Creek. At the admission of Kansas as a state in 1861, making it the thirty-fourth state, the first legislature passed the first game protection law. Consisting of thirty-eight words, it stated "that it is unlawful for person or persons to shoot, kill, or trap within this state any prairie chicken, quail, partridge, wild turkey, and deer between the first days of April and September of each year." The fine was not to exceed five dollars. There were no wardens to enforce the law. The first fish laws were established in 1883. Additional laws were passed in 1886, and the position of game warden was not created until 1895. The first wardens were nonpaid and appointed in each county. They were empowered to make arrests and would be compensated five dollars for each conviction along with the regular "constable" travel allowance. The warden would travel by horse, buggy or railcar.

In 1900, the first full-time fish warden was George W. Wiley. Under his leadership, in 1901, the Kansas legislature appropriated $2,800 for fish propagation and protection. In 1905, the merger of fisheries and wildlife protection occurred. The title state fish warden was changed to state fish and game warden. This position paid $1,500 per year. The first hunting licenses were required in 1905, along with bag limits. It was not until 1921 that the governor authorized the state game warden to appoint six special state deputy game wardens. In 1923 an eighteen-foot keel boat was purchased to patrol and enforce regulations on streams in the state. The ten-dollar fines were put into the Fish and Game Fee Fund and used to purchase the first patrol vehicles. Four Ford coupes and a Hudson Coach were purchased, and an extra engine was kept at the Pratt Fish Hatchery when needed.

The first tragedy came in January 1925, when part-time deputy F.W. Tierney was shot and killed near Wilburton. This was the year when non-residents were required to obtain fishing licenses. In 1927, the Forestry, Fish and Game Commission gained full control over the department. There was a staff of 10 state deputy game wardens and 375

Kansas game wardens. *Courtesy of Major Dan Hesket, Kansas Department of Wildlife, Parks, and Tourism.*

unsalaried county game wardens. A turning point for the department occurred when the Federal Aid in Wildlife Restoration Act provided a 10 percent excise tax on sporting arms and ammunition, and those funds were appropriated to the states.

In 1939, there were ninety-three sportsman's organizations in the 105 counties and nearly three thousand game protectors appointed on the recommendation of the license holders. Under the leadership of Dave Leahy, appointed director, from 1944 to 1960 some young men coming back from the war were hired as state game protectors. The group worked, and the numbers of wildlife grew substantially. The protectors were very loyal to their director. Several state lakes and federal reservoirs were constructed during this period and added substantially to the workload of the staff. In 1958, the United States Coast Guard enacted the Boating Safety Act, and the commission was authorized to enforce the regulations.

The Kansas State Parks Department was responsible for enforcing regulations in the parks area but for many years did not commission law enforcement officers. In 1987, under Governor Mike Hayden, the Kansas

Fish and Game Commission was merged with the Kansas State Park and Resource Authority. Also, Kansas tourism interests were transferred from the Department of Commerce to this office. This allowed for the combined law enforcement unit trained and commissioned by the state. Today, the combined offices of the department work on hatcheries and provide biological and law enforcement work to maintain safety and a great outdoor experience for the citizens and visitors of Kansas. Today, the official name of the department is the Kansas Department of Wildlife, Parks and Tourism.

ALTA MILL

Alta is located on the Little Arkansas River, about eight miles northwest of Newton, or just south of Moundridge. Joseph Schrag and Jacob Gering bought a twelve-acre mill site in 1876 and built the first mill on the east side of the river. In 1878, a brush dam was built across the river and a millrace constructed. The millrace was parallel to the river. River water was diverted into the millrace, which passed closer to the mill and provided power for the turbine water wheel. A small dam at the end of the race controlled the water through the flow gate.

A twenty-three-inch steel water turbine produced power to operate the burr and the machinery of the mill. Just above the turbine was a brush trap to screen out branches and trash and also a flow gate that could be opened and closed by a six-inch cable and winch. A trough directed the stream of water onto the turbine to turn it. This turbine rested on a wooden bearing that never needed replacing during its forty years of use.

In the spring of 1885, the old brush dam was washed out during high water. It was removed, and John J. Schrag built a hollow wooden dam that lasted thirty-three years. It was washed out in 1918 when it was undermined by muskrats.

A second mill was built on the east side of the river by Peter J. Claassen. It was a three-story block building. A belt transmitted power from the turbine to the machinery in the new building. A five-roller mill replaced the old burr mill. A steam engine was added to power the mill when there was not enough water in the fall. A gasoline engine was added in 1907.

There was a flood in 1905. The Claassen mill withstood the flood, but the basement filled, causing more than $1,000 of damage to wheat and machinery. The miller's house had fourteen inches of water on the floors inside. The barn floated off its foundation. Not wanting to face a similar situation again, Claassen sold the mill to a group of farmers and investors from Moundridge and Buhler and then moved to Newton.

The new ownership became the Alta Milling Company. John E. Stucky and Jacob J. Stucky were trained by Claassen to manage the mill. The two managed the business for many years for the group.

There was considerable pressure during World War I in the Mennonite community about their pacifist views, and there were several instances of mob action over the purchase of war bonds. Purchasing war bonds was considered by the group as a violation of their faith tenets and supported the war. There were several instances of putting yellow paint, tar and feathers on members who refused to buy the war bonds.

After John Schrag was arrested and went to trial in federal court in Wichita, he was acquitted and the actions slowed down. The Schrags were asked what they did about the war bonds. The answer was that they were too old to be drafted and were not asked to buy the bonds. However, one day an army truck pulled up in front of the mill and started loading flour sacks. When they protested, they were told that this was their contribution to the war effort. After cooling off, John noted that "soldiers had to eat too."

Farmers came from as far away as Meade to have their wheat ground into flour at the Alta mill. In 1949, the corporation dissolved. The mill was sold and torn down by Jake Schrag. Some of the machinery was taken to the Goessel Wheat Museum, where it remains on display.

ANTHONY BENTON GUDE

When Anthony Benton Gude went to art school, he did not tell anyone who his grandfather was. Wanting to build his talent on his own, he did not want the added notoriety or pressure of being Thomas Hart Benton's grandson. It did not take long for those instructing him and those viewing his work to see a technique that struck a familiar note.

Anthony was the son of Jesse Benton's daughter. He was born on Martha's Vineyard and grew up around his grandfather's work and in his studios, especially the one in Kansas. The farm in Kansas was a place that he would visit as a child, finding a space that captured the same vision his grandfather had. The influence had to be something that set Anthony on his journey as an artist and a lover of the country.

Anthony's work captures the everyday scenes that typify the Kansas countryside and way of life. He remembered watching his grandfather paint but did not remember any conversations with him about art. Thomas Hart Benton died when Anthony was twelve. He remembered enjoying his grandfather's company very much. He also recalled a long line of actors, writers, artists and politicians coming to visit him. Some names included Walter Cronkite and author James Thurber.

By the time Anthony was twenty-one, he was working in the construction business, matching paints and doing renderings of building projects. This caused his mother to suggest he enroll in art school. He had been drawing all his life and was painting just for fun. He did not realize that he was pretty good until he was in art school. He chose to study at the School of the Museum of Fine Arts in Boston. He focused on learning the skills of the old masters, how to stretch canvas and make gesso and glue. He also studied at the Art Students League in New York City and learned the techniques he uses today. His focus was on drawing and anatomy; he wanted to be an expert on drawing the human figure.

Anthony generally works in oil, but he also likes water color and egg tempera. He said that he never runs out of ideas for his works. Beginning in 1986, he was commissioned to do a mural for the *Marysville Advocate*, the local newspaper. This led to a show at an art gallery in the Union Hill District of Kansas City, Missouri. He sold out his first show.

In 1996, Anthony made the Marysville farm his home base, and four years later, he built a studio with natural light that was large enough to handle his full-size murals. The murals are done in sections and transported to the locations where they are installed. His most elaborate mural came in the 1990s for the St. Joseph Riverboat Partners in St. Joseph, Missouri.

Tagged as a "regionalist," Anthony does two art shows a year, and his grandfather's influence can be seen in his works, although he is his own creative spirit and captures the Kansas countryside in a unique fashion. Through his many murals and individual paintings, Anthony captures a piece of the rural spirit that will stand beside Thomas Hart Benton's works and inspire artists for generations to come.

AUTO-FEDAN HAY PRESS COMPANY

Edward P. Ross was born in Princeton, Illinois, on December 8, 1863. In 1870, the family moved to Emporia, Kansas. Ross spent five or six years in New Mexico. He was in the real estate business and farmed. He came back to St. John, Kansas, to engage in these occupations. Ross's first business venture was in the hay business, and he came to realize that there needed to be a better way to package hay for handling and sale. He set out to improve the hay presses of the time. The result was the Auto-Fedan Hay Press.

Ross began to manufacture the press in small quantities in Emporia and Topeka. As the demand grew, the facilities in those two cities were outgrown, and he moved to Rosedale. In 1908, he organized the company and was the president. The business really took off, and soon he had offices in Kansas City, Kansas, and later moved them to Kansas City, Missouri.

At the time, there were many companies building and selling hay presses, but the Auto-Fedan outsold them all and was shipped all over the world. Company representatives went out to organize large uses of the hay presses. A story in the *Junction City Daily Union* tells the tale of J.A. Ross, a

An advertisement for the Auto-Fedan Hay Press. *Courtesy of Newpapers.com.*

member of the company, setting up eight hay presses on a reservation with Ed Whitehair. At the hay camps besides eight hay presses there were eight eight-foot Emerson Mowers laying down the hay, each mower cutting an average of twenty acres per day.

The Auto-Fedan Hay Press Company had an aggressive sales team, and advertisements were found nationwide pushing the hay press. At the Kansas City Manufacturers Exposition of 1912, the Auto-Fedan Company offices were listed at 1521 West Twelfth Street in Kansas City, Missouri. The early presses were powered by belt, with horsepower providing the energy. Stationary engines could be adapted later on, and eventually tractors would be able to power the presses. The company stressed that the feeder attachment separated this press from the others on the market.

The *Encyclopedia of American Farm Implements and Antiques* by C.H. Wendel shows that 181 hay presses were manufactured in the United States from 1882 to 1922. A large number of companies started around the same time as the Auto-Fedan. The competition was huge, and it had to be a really great press to have the sales that it did.

Edward Ross married Miss Alice Goodhue of Topeka in 1905. They were avid golfers and became avid motorists. There are still Auto-Fedan Hay Presses in working order used and displayed by collectors and enthusiasts at shows nationwide.

BUCKSKIN JOE

Maybe you have heard of Buckskin Joe if you are from the Arkansas City area, but here is one character that probably lived the adventures that the movies and Wild West novels made up. He was born in Canada, and the story of his growing up is almost too unbelievable. One would think that it was taken and enhanced by a promotion agent.

Buckskin Joe was born near Magog, Canada, Province of Quebec, on October 4, 1840, and the family lived in a log cabin in the shadow of Mount Orford. His parents, Samuel and Judith, named him Edward Jonathan. His early life was fraught with danger, living in a wilderness inhabited by Indians and wild animals. When he was one year old, his mother left him in the cabin and went out to milk the cow. He soon put up a howl to accompany a squealing noise, and a wild hog was discovered in the cabin, with Joe in its jaws and running off. His mother took after them and threw the milk stool, hitting the hog. The hog squealed and dropped Joe, with just some clothing left over in its jaws.

As a boy, Joe was full of mischief and was always into some adventure. The school board finally visited the schoolmarm and convinced her that the punishments for Joe were not nearly severe enough. After a good licking with a switch, Joe thanked her, kicked the stove pipe down and went out the window, as he had many times before. Joe took a stagecoach across the Canada/U.S. border and caught a train to Boston. He boarded a freighter and worked his way around Cape Horn to the California gold fields. He was met at the dock by a family member and went back to Canada, but not back to school.

He went to work in a lumber camp of his father's and became a quite accomplished athlete. He joined his grandfather, who was an old trapper, and went to the woods to live among the Indians. He took up their habits and clothing, thus gaining the moniker "Buckskin." He learned how to live like them, and his grandfather taught him to use a gun and knife and drink the "hot toddy."

Joe joined the J.T. Johnson Wagon Circus and toured the eastern part of the United States. He learned to be an aerialist and mastered several instruments, becoming quite accomplished in music and soon even instructing others.

When the Civil War began, he joined the Union army. Now known as "Buckskin Joe," he was with the Army of the Potomac under General George B. McClellan in the First Battle of Bull Run. He was in so many battles that he admitted losing track of them. After the war, he returned to the circus. He began walking along strands of wire stretched between buildings in the cities where they performed. He had a signed contract to walk across the Royal Gorge at one time, but there is no evidence that he did. He tumbled and amazed crowds and would demonstrate extraordinary feats with a bow and arrow.

Joe ended up in the West working as a scout under Captain C.M. Scott and was one of the first to settle his family at Arkansas City. Things were pretty rough on the plains and there was no relief from the government, so he decided to fake the threat of Indians going on the warpath. First he fired on the Indians and then rode into town warning of imminent attack. He organized home guard companies and got the governor to pay them for their services.

In the 1870s, Joe went to the Colorado gold fields. A silver strike drew him to Leadville. He sank twenty-two mine shafts and made several men millionaires from his discoveries. He survived numerous claim jumpers and was a troubleshooter for Colorado's Silver King. He explored the Gunnison and Cripple Creek areas and founded Glenwood Springs. He was there during the Ute Indian uprising in 1879.

Joe guided wagon trains across Kansas to Colorado and the Western Slope. He always came back to his family in Arkansas City. He organized a Wild West Orchestra called the Border Brass Band and a family Cow Horn Band, which Pawnee Bill added to his Wild West Show. He made cow horns into instruments, which made the band sound like a calliope. He served as a deputy U.S. marshal for the federal court of Wichita over Indian Territory, toured with his own show, raced in the opening of the Cherokee Strip and went to the jungles of Honduras. Joe was described by a grandson as a "Superman."

EMANUEL HALDEMAN-JULIUS: HERO/ANTIHERO

If you ever happen upon copies of small blue books—not just in bookstores or libraries but in many other unusual places—they are the product of Emanuel Haldeman-Julius and were produced in Girard. Depending on your point of view, he would be a hero or antihero. If there is any person in Kansas history full of contradictions, it would be Emanuel. Even his death has ignited a firestorm of curiosity and polarized opinions. Let's go through the facts.

Emanuel was a most prolific publisher, with an estimated 300 million copies of the "Little Blue Books." He is credited in bringing literature to millions at extremely affordable prices. Subjects that were not allowed in public libraries and other controversial topics were included in the titles, as well as introducing writers such as Will Durant, Bertrand Russell and Clarence Darrow to the American public. The books were small and designed so that the workingman could carry a copy in his pants pocket. The books even had the approval and recommendation of Ethiopian emperor Hailie Selassie and were carried to the South Pole by Admiral Richard Byrd.

Who was Emanuel and how did he get to Girard? Emanuel was born in Philadelphia in 1889, the son of Russian-Jewish parents who had immigrated to America from Odessa. The family's name was Zolajefsky and was simplified by his father. His father found work as a book binder, and young Emanuel became fascinated by books at an early age. At age thirteen, he quit school to become an usher at the Keith Theater and later a bellboy at Miss Mason's School for Girls. What money was left from helping the family he put into books. At age fifteen, he bought a dime copy of Oscar Wilde's "The Ballad of Reading Gaol." Later, that would be one of the titles he would publish. It was during this time that he read an article in the *International Socialists Review*. It appealed to his heart, and he sold his first article to that journal for ten dollars, starting his writing career.

Emanuel went to many large papers in the next few years. Landing in New York, he found the Socialist scene in Greenwich Village and made friends in the community. Louis Kopelin offered Emanuel a large pay raise to come to Kansas and write for the *Appeal to Reason*, a Socialist paper that printed more copies per week than the Sunday edition of the *New York Times*. *Appeal to Reason* was an odd publication to be found in Kansas, but the ability to send mail orders out was a major reason for its location, as well as the large immigrant population that had come to the area to work the mines in southeast Kansas. Along with the cost of living, this prompted J.A. Wayland to bring his paper and publishing company to Girard. Here he found a willing and large labor force available.

Emanuel was described as an atheist-Jew, Socialist and newspaper publisher. His views on sexuality, birth control and socialism kept him in trouble with the government, and at the time of his death, he was looking at spending six months in prison. His wife, Marcet Haldeman, was an aspiring actress. She had returned to Girard to attend her mother's funeral and was set to inherit her father's bank. Marcet was not what local people were used to—she was independent, smoked cigarettes and was educated at Bryn Mawr. After a courtship of six months, they entered a "companionment marriage" (an arrangement that embraced independence, balanced responsibilities and birth control). After the wedding, Emanuel formally took Marcet's name, so it appears as Emanuel Haldeman-Julius. Together they purchased the publishing company from Kopelin.

The Blue Books system took books whose copyright had expired, so they were in the public domain, and printed the titles. He offered the books to the 175,000 subscribers of *Appeal to Reason*. The original fifty-book series was offered for five dollars, and five thousand orders soon showed up. He diverted his energies into creating more titles for the series and publishing more books. His goal was to create books that could be read by all people, rich or poor. Along with the classic titles, more radical titles were also introduced.

His flair for promotion and innovation allowed him to cut the cost per copy to produce and lower the retail cost so more people could afford the books. The fifty- to sixty-page books were produced with blue covers, and even though he did use other colors, the series was always known as the Little Blue Books.

With the success of mail order, Emanuel started to set up franchise stores across the continent, including Boston, Buffalo, Atlantic City, Montreal, Cincinnati, Milwaukee, Atlanta, San Francisco and Portland. The Los Angeles store placed an order for 250,000 copies. Books were sold in vending machines. In the end, the mail-order business sold the bulk of the books.

Emanuel commented on his business:

> *If you make the low brow believe that Ibsen, Shaw, Voltaire, Emerson, and other rather forbidding persons are human beings with a very human appeal, they will buy readily, because the name means nothing. They do not buy the name of the author but buy the suggestion that the material in the book will interest them. Too much effort cannot be expended in making it clear to modern readers that when Aristophanes, Sophocles, and Euripides, for example, wrote their powerful dramas, that appealed to their people not because they were writing great plays but because they depicted life in a manner that the Greeks of their day could recognize and understand.*

The *St. Louis Post-Dispatch* called Emanuel "the Henry Ford of literature." Others would dub him as the "Book Baron," "Voltaire from Kansas" and the "Barnum of Books."

From the 1920s through the Depression, the Little Blue Books would be found in hospital wards, factory break rooms, prison cells, in the back pockets of workers and handed from one person to another. Some believe that they brought education to the common man and pushed the standards of education in public schools. Some titles foreshadowed the sexual revolution and found their way into the hands of the civil rights movement. W.E.B. Du Bois recommended the Little Blue Books in *The Crisis*. The books became a tool for the self-educated and were found in the more radical communities of the country. Langston Hughes and Claude McKay were strongly influenced by the books.

Emanuel and his wife moved into a big white house complete with a backyard swimming pool on a farm outside Girard. They raised a son and daughter there and entertained a steady flow of well-known guests that included Upton Sinclair, Clarence Darrow, Anna Louise Strong and Will Durant. As a cigar enthusiast, Emanuel rose every morning to smoke and sort through mail orders. He was fond of noting that some of his best customers were Charlie Chaplin, Gloria Swanson and Franklin P. Adams, as well as Haile Selassie of Abyssinia. Despite their strong professional bonds and lifestyle similarities, Emanuel and Marcet divorced. Both suffered from alcoholism.

Emanuel took refuge from his domestic complications in Chicago and New York. He produced no new titles after 1931 but managed to keep the workers employed due to the stream of mail orders. Marcet left the house to him when she died from cancer, and Emanuel moved in with his second wife, Sue.

Emanuel cultivated enemies from all quarters because of his anti-religious and anti-corporate stances. Letter writing campaigns and postcards from detractors were sent to newspapers and magazines that advertised the Little Blue Books series. Editorials were printed encouraging people to not read or buy the books, but none of this stopped him from publishing.

When Emanuel published a book called *The FBI: Alarming Methods of J. Edgar Hoover*, Hoover and the Federal Bureau of Investigation responded vigorously. The IRS took an interest in his printing operation and sued him for $120,000 in unpaid taxes going back to 1945. Sue had noticed that he had been collecting information on Mexico. The courts found him guilty of tax evasion. He was fined $12,500 and sentenced to six months in jail. This came during a time when the Cold War was heating up, and there was a lot of worry about threats to the nation. In the earliest years, two works that were now coming back to haunt him were the *Communist Manifesto* and the Soviet Constitution.

On July 31, 1951, Emanuel was found floating in his swimming pool. There was much speculation that he had been killed for his views on Socialism and his independent style. The event made national news. The local coroner suspected suicide, yet the note found for his wife was not a suicide note, but a joke. Many believed he was killed for being a Soviet spy. We will never know the true circumstances of his death.

There is a small marker in Girard that marks the fact that a huge printing industry thrived there, and its existence is known mostly by locals and collectors.

DRAINING THE McPHERSON WETLANDS

The McPherson Wetlands stretched from near Conway to near Valley Center. As settlement and agriculture started to crowd the area, there was a desire to drain the wetlands and turn them into farm fields. There were many downsides to the area for farmers from the fluctuating water levels pushing into farm fields and buildings and pushing animal pests out of the swamps into the fields. Another problem was from drowned animals caught in sudden water risings and the stench from the decomposing bodies. There also was a problem maintaining access from one part of the county to another.

Although there was some opposition to the drainage, the idea caught on, and the man to drain them, John J. Schrag, was a Mennonite who was a natural and self-trained engineer as well as a farmer. Schrag lived in Harvey County and had helped his father build the Alta Vista flour mill. He designed and built the dam to fill the water race that diverted water to run the mill. He created a bush and soil dam that worked well but had to be replaced an average of three years after high water. He designed a wooden dam later that lasted for years.

Schrag agreed to drain Big Basin and started to buy properties of the area. His plan was to build dikes around the larger parts of the acreage and build drainage ditches around the outside of the dikes. The dikes were built to drain the water into Blaze Fork Creek. He accomplished the dike construction with a large diker, which was similar to the powered terracing machines of today.

The ditches were built with horse-drawn slips and Fresnos, which worked well until the sides became too high for the horses to work. On the basin's south edge was a hill that was a fifteen-foot rise to dig through, and conventional methods were not enough. The job required a steam shovel. Steam shovels were expensive, however, and there was not one available remotely near the project. So, using his engineering skills and imagination, he built his own.

The steam shovel was as unique as anyone could have imagined, as it was made from cottonwood logs. He cut down trees and cut off eighteen-inch-thick sections for wheels. He would bore the centers for insertion of axels. On this was built a platform, and the steam engine was mounted to the platform. Movement of the shovel would be accomplished with four winches. Since there was no drive train, hedge posts were set one hundred feet from the shovel, and when the unit needed to be moved, it was pulled with a block and tackle.

The sum of his actions effectively blocked twenty thousand acres of surface water and diverted water into the Blaze Fork. Farmers alongside the Schrag ditches built their own ditches and dammed Schrag's ditch. This created a lawsuit. Schrag won the lawsuit in district court, lost the suit in appeals court and won the suit in a Kansas Supreme Court decision. Two years after winning the lawsuit, John retired and deeded the land over to his children. At that time, Peter J. Schrag and his brothers became active in the Big Basin project.

The Schrags had agreed to increase the capacity of the drainage ditches. The simple method used to enlarge the ditches at low cost was to plow the bottoms and let the water flow carry the loose soil away. Others started purchasing land and draining it as well, so it was no longer just a Schrag project. Drainage District no. 4 was formed in 1948. In 1952, the Blaze Fork Drainage District and Drainage District no. 4 agreed to do annual maintenance to the ditches and to communicate and agree on work to be done.

This agreement survives today. But there is a new addition to the story. It has been recognized by many people that the draining of the wetlands was not a very good idea. There are still crop losses during high-water periods, and the negative impact on wildlife has been recognized on a wide scale. An agreement with Kansas Wildlife, Parks and Tourism and organizations such as Ducks Unlimited and the Nature Conservancy acknowledges that an effort to restore the wetlands would be good for the public and wildlife.

By buying property from willing sellers and bringing back the portions of the historic wetlands, there is great promise. Today, you can go out and catch a glimpse of what the original wetlands looked like. There are observation platforms and areas that are handicap accessible.

OMC TRACTOR: OSTENBERG MOTOR PARTS COMPANY

The Ostenberg brothers grew up and lived in Smolan. They went into business together and owned the Ostenberg Motor Company in Salina. The company was in the machine shop and parts business, as well as being an agricultural equipment dealership. The brothers started selling automotive parts in 1918. There were times in the winter that business slowed down, and the idea for a new product to sell started to germinate.

In the late 1930s, the tractor revolution in farm equipment was in full swing, and since the 1910s, there had been a large number of companies and individuals that tried to build the next best farm tractor. The brothers did the same. In the 1930s, they started to build the OMC tractor, which used mostly component parts from off the shelf. F. Amos Ostenberg was a very mechanically minded man and developed a new type of frame for the tractor that made it much stronger and easier to build.

The company built a handful of tractors in 1939—the number ranges from six to eight. The Ostenberg tractor used a commercial Chrysler engine and a heavy-duty five-speed transmission. The frame was an original design from the company.

Production stopped for World War II, but the company was back in production by 1946. These tractors did not have a standard serial number, so it is difficult to identify years of production for models of those tractors that still exist. The tractor resembled the Allis Chalmers WD and was originally designed with rubber tires.

A problem arose with a Canadian company when it started to produce the Norseman tractor, based on the Ostenberg design. Ostenberg thought he had an agreement that the Norseman could be built as a franchise and that he would receive royalties for his design. This did not happen. Although Ostenberg held a patent on the frame design, because the rest of the tractor was off-the-shelf components, it was not subject to any royalties. It is not known why there was no litigation over the use of the patented frame.

Just as the OMC was a pretty good tractor that filled a void in available tractors during this time, the Norseman never generated enough sales to keep the Canadian company in business very long. The Ostenberg factory burned down in 1954, and that spelled the end of the OMC. All company records were destroyed in the factory fire, so there is very little known about this little tractor other than the survivors.

The Ostenberg brothers went on to other business ventures in their life. F. Amos was active in community affairs and in real estate. Luther, who was known as "Lute," became a Ford and Durant dealer and was the general manager of the Salina Blue Jays semipro baseball team. The Blue Jays were a part of the Philadelphia Phillies baseball system.

F. Amos was always bitter about the Canadian company building his tractor, but since there was only a verbal agreement, he could not do much about the infringement. The patent was not apparently received or applied for on the tractor frame in Canada, and it is possible that the lawsuit needed to

The OMC tractor, built in Salina, Kansas. Ostenberg Motor Company. *Courtesy of Irvin Priest.*

get compensation would have been too expensive. Also, since the Norseman did not become a big seller, there was nothing to justify the expense and time needed to complete a lawsuit.

Luther died in 1964 at sixty-four years of age. F. Amos died in 1980. Both brothers are buried at the Gypsum Hill Cemetery in Saline County.

SINKHOLE SAM

Kansas has had few legends that reached a national and international level. In the 1950s, just southeast of Inman, in an area that is full of sinkholes, a couple of fishermen claimed that they saw a creature that was unlike anything that had been seen in Kansas—or anywhere else.

The two fishermen's names have been lost to time, and maybe for good reason. It is thought that the pair had spent some time in a local establishment before going out to the sinkhole near Lake Inman. When the pair rushed back to town, they brought with them a story of sighting a creature that had a big, flat head with teeth and a body about fifteen feet long and about twenty-some inches in diameter, and it was black. They compared the diameter of the body to a car tire.

Soon a reporter by the name of Mary Kay Flynn had a story on the newswire telling the story of the creature's sighting and the excitement that it had created. The creature was soon named "Sinkhole Sam." Papers around the country picked up the story along with a photo of the sinkhole where the sighting was supposed to have occurred.

People soon came by the hundreds to try and get a glimpse of the creature. A local man named Albert Neufeld claimed to have put a couple of .22-caliber shots into Sam with no effect. Later, George Reiger Jr. was standing on the bridge and claimed that he saw Sam and that further shots had no effect on him.

Fishermen shied away from the area, but droves of people came for the chance to see him. In a later article, it was stated that two "great scientific minds" were brought in by the names of Ernest Dewey and Dr. Erasmus P. Quattlebaum. The men pronounced Sam to be a foopengerkle, one of the extinctest creatures to ever inhabit the plains. According to the story, Sam became Sam rather than Samantha because female foopengerkles never existed. In the final report, the "expert" warned that Sam did not seem to realize that he was extinct.

In the November 23, 1952 *Salina Journal*, Ernest Dewey wrote that the unknown monster was "a plain old Foopengerkle." He claimed that he and his assistant, Dr. Erasmus P. Quattlebaum, had examined the little evidence at the big sinkhole.

Mr. Dewey went on to explain that the foopengerkles disappeared as the state became civilized, and since there was no apparent use for the species, it diminished. He also proclaimed the species to be particularly stupid. Since there were no female foopengerkles, the males at mating season got excited but were too dumb to know why. The species dug deep holes in ponds just to kill time and burrowed deep down. Since it is an extinct species, there is the possibility that occasionally one may come up to look at people just to see what they have become. He goes on to warn that the species is vegetarian but that caution should be taken since he may forget that he is vegetarian. His final statement was that since the country had become Republican, the foopengerkle might just disappear altogether.

In researching the "scientific experts," I found that Ernest Dewey had been on the radio at KIMV 94.5 FM in Hutchinson and had regular columns in local newspapers. It seems that his evaluation may have been tongue-in-cheek. The consultant Dr. Erasmus P. Quattlebaum

Artist rendering of the legend of Sinkhole Sam. *Courtesy of Martha Brohammer.*

was harder to locate, but the Quattlebaum name is a legitimate name. Of the hundreds of Quattlebaums I checked out, I found no record of an Erasmus who was listed as being an ophiologist. Ernest Dewey did confess that he has only seen two foopengerkles in his lifetime, and his grandkids don't believe him. He said that the people who did see Sam are fortunate, as they will have stories to tell their grandkids who also won't believe them.

The sinkhole is located at the famous Section 27, which author and farmer Mil Penner wrote about in his family history of the site. The offices of the Kansas Sampler Foundation are located by the homestead on the south side. If you are in the area southeast of Inman and happen by the Kansas Sampler offices, you may want to stop in and ask Marci about the famous Sinkhole Sam. She has become a bit of an expert on foopengerkles herself.

CASH HOLLISTER: CALDWELL LAWMAN

Caldwell has a very interesting history being right on the Chisholm Trail and on the border with Indian Territory. It became one of the late bloomers in the cattle trade for the same reason that Dodge City also was a little later in the timeline: the movement having to do with the advancing enforcement of the quarantine laws stopping Texas cattle from being brought through areas that were being settled. The main reason was the spread of the Texas Fever to domestic cattle. This was before the discovery that the fever that killed all northern cattle was actually carried by a tick to which the carrier Longhorns were immune.

The other reason that Caldwell and Hunnewell became important in the cattle trade were the railroads reaching south to the Indian Territory border. The town of Caldwell had a rowdy element from the start, and law enforcement was a very hazardous occupation. It was where the very competent and well-liked Mike Meagher, former sheriff of Sedgwick County, was killed.

Cassius M. "Cash" Hollister was born in Cleveland, Ohio, on December 7, 1845. Cash moved to Kansas in 1877 and worked as a hotel clerk in Wichita and Caldwell. He lived in Caldwell and married Sadie Rhodes, later becoming elected mayor after the sudden death of the town's first mayor, Noah J. Dixon.

Cash was known to be a bit rowdy and was involved in several fistfights. He was arrested for assault, for which he was fined one dollar. He continued with some street fighting and minor legal problems. He was suspended as mayor because of his fighting. Then fate put Cash in the role that was suited for him, maybe due to his toughness. In 1883, Cash was appointed to be a deputy U.S. marshal by B.S. Simpson and soon assisted in the capture of horse thief Frank Horstetter, who was connected to a major cattle rustling ring in Arkansas City. The ringleader, Jay Wilkinson, escaped before the arrest.

On April 8, 1883, Cash was involved in a large gunfight with Caldwell Marshal Henry Brown, Ben Wheeler and several others near Hunnewell against a gang of cattle rustlers, killing one outlaw and wounding another. Cash also investigated a murder in Indian Territory and brought back several suspects.

On November 21, 1883, a report arrived of one Chet van Meter living on a farm in Chikaskia Township who had beaten on his wife and fired at his neighbors. He swore that he "would kill half a dozen of them before he would be through." An arrest warrant was sworn out against Van Meter, and Cash was authorized to bring him in. He was advised that Van Meter was armed and to anticipate trouble. He arrived at Van Meter's home and found him gone. Van Meter had gone to his father's house about five miles away. Accompanied by Ben Wheeler, Cash made his way to the father's home. They called for his surrender, and just as he seemed to comply, he raised his rifle, taking a shot at Cash. Both deputies returned fire, hitting Van Meter a total of seven times and killing him. Chet van Meter was brought to Caldwell and placed in the front basement of the Leland Hotel, where an inquest by a coroner's jury was called. The ruling was that the shooting was justified.

Resigning as U.S. marshal the following year, Cash remained a deputy sheriff of Sumner County. He was called on October 18, 1884, to arrest a Texas outlaw who had kidnapped the daughter of a local farmer. Robert Cross refused to surrender to Deputy Cash and fatally shot him when he threatened to set fire to the house he was in. Cross was arrested by authorities two days later. An article in the Augusta newspaper stated "that authorities were trying to keep ahead of a lynch mob who was intent on hanging the killer of Cash Hollister." The entire town turned out for Cash Hollister's funeral. He had served as mayor, U.S. deputy marshal, Sumner County deputy sheriff and Caldwell city marshal. He was married to Sadie Rhodes, the daughter of Mr. and Mrs. Abram Rhodes. He left behind his wife and a five-year-old son.

The City of Caldwell conducts tours in the cemetery north of town of the graves of prominent citizens and local characters from its history. There is a tall headstone at the grave of C.M. Hollister. Hollister is memorialized at Panel 40, E-6, on the National Law Enforcement Officers Memorial in Washington, D.C.

GEORGE GRANT: MR. ANGUS

If you go to the cemetery in Victoria, you will find a small park with a monument to Mr. George Grant, who was the first to import Aberdeen Angus bulls to the United States. As renowned as the man is, it is again hard to make your way through the legend and get to the true story of who he was. He is celebrated, and for good measure, for the establishment of a cattle breed that is now a major factor in beef production in both

Kansas and the United States. He was a forward-thinking man and an astute businessman.

George Grant was born in Scotland on April 28, 1878. He had received worldwide recognition as a successful silk merchant in London, England, and gained considerable wealth in other ventures. Stepping off the train in Hays City, a romantic vision was offered by Marjorie Gamet Raish in her book *Victoria: The Story of a Western Kansas Town*. Historians are quick to add doubt to this, as his quest was to create a colony owned by British immigrants along the Kansas Pacific Railroad route and Big Creek and its North Fork.

Being the promoter that he was, Grant brought along Mr. Collins, a member of the English press. He was also accompanied by Mr. J. Jaroslauski, city financial correspondent for the New York German newspapers. He was seeking capital from both England and the United States to achieve his goals. He intended to build a town named for the queen of England and build a manor house for himself. The house that is listed in the National Register of Historic Places is purported to be the house he built, but there is some discrepancy in the story even though he did live in the home.

The acreage amounts that Grant acquired varied so much that it is difficult to ascertain what they actually were. Reports of the size of his holdings for his large-scale British cattle and sheep farm changed each time they were reported in a new newspaper. In 1872, the amounts reported went from 40,000 to 50,000 to 60,000 acres. The *Kansas City Journal* reported in May 1873 that the month the first colonists arrived, the water frontage of the Victoria Colony traversed two hundred miles. Later, the *Kansas City Journal of Commerce* reported that Grant had purchased 300,000 acres, or nearly five hundred square miles of territory.

The newspaper reports are exaggerated and led other papers to start a war of words with the competitors. Some reports had Grant's holdings as the largest privately owned ranch in the country. Regardless of the hype of the papers of the time, a huge cattle and sheep operation was established and covered a massive area. It was reported that stock had grazed railroad land, other property owners' lands and government land. Grant's vision was not to work out in the way he had planned. Most of the settlers who had moved out to the Victoria area went back to Europe, and his investors did not come forth in sufficient numbers. Yet Grant imported four Aberdeen Angus bulls, establishing the breed for the first time on U.S. soil. In showing two bulls at the Kansas City Livestock

Memorial to Mr. George Grant "Mr. Angus" in Victoria, Kansas. *Courtesy of Carol Schuteze.*

Exhibition, the initial reaction was that the polled cattle (naturally no horns) with black coloring were freaks. Shorthorns and Longhorns were the predominant cattle at the time. Grant crossbred the Angus bulls with Longhorn cows and raised polled black calves that gained twice as fast as the Longhorn purebreds and tolerated the winter weather better than other breeds.

George Grant died south of Victoria on April 28, 1878, and is buried at the Victoria Cemetery. A monument was erected near his burial site by the Aberdeen Angus Association commemorating the arrival of the Angus breed in the United States on May 17, 1873. On May 17, 1973, the association had a rededication of the monument, capping it with a replica of an Angus bull. Improvements to the park were made with the addition of paved sidewalks, benches and planting trees. On September 27, 2008, the monument restoration was unveiled to commemorate the 135th anniversary of the arrival of the Angus breed and the 125th anniversary of the Aberdeen Angus Association. When George Grant died, it took many years to untangle the acreage that he had acquired, and there were still title clouds on some real estate until the 1950s. For all the words written, George had a profound effect on the state of Kansas and the United States beef industry. Visitors can go to the monument whenever they visit Victoria.

JACOB JOHN "INDIAN JOHN" DERRINGER

"Indian John" Derringer became a legendary figure who has been cloaked in mystery. He lived in many locations, but mostly near Fact, which is northeast of Clay Center. He was widely known for his herbal medicines and sold a remedy for many aliments. People suffering from various ailments sent for his cures. Many would send personal items from which he would "diagnose" their illnesses and then send them his prescription.

His tombstone at the Idyllwild Cemetery lists his name as Jacob John Derringer, born in 1832 and died in 1924. The story was that he was three-quarters Sioux. Childhood accounts vary, however. Some believe that he was part Sioux and part French. Others say he was born on an Ohio homestead, ran away from home when he was fifteen, was kidnapped by a Sioux hunting party and then was rescued by the cavalry and sent home to Ohio.

Why he was in Kansas in 1854 is unknown. Some researchers and firsthand accounts indicate that he was a scout for General Custer in the 1860s and worked with rail crews that were laying track across Kansas and Colorado.

Indians who came into contact with John thought that he had special healing powers and taught him herbal medicine, according to an article by Dr. Carl Nelson in the September 10, 1981 edition of the *Waterville Telegraph*. Gale Wolenberg, who wrote two volumes on John, believes that John's tutor was Joseph Napoleon Bourassa, a Potawatomie living near Union Town in Shawnee County who was known as Joseph Makes Good Medicine. Bourassa attended Hamilton College and then law school in Kentucky. He was instructor for a while at Choctaw Academy and then came to the Kansas Territory in the 1840s. By the late 1860s, Bourassa was holding regular classes teaching herbal medicine, and in 1868, John began to receive instruction.

John left Kansas for a while and returned in the 1870s; he began traveling northeastern Kansas treating people. He moved to a farm near Kimeo in Washington County. He would put ten to fifteen patients in a semicircle without anyone saying anything and tell each one what was wrong with them and what medicine to take.

John was tall and had long hair. He gathered herbs in the fall from the prairie, pastures and creek banks. He would cook them in an iron kettle outside his house. Most of his medicine was kept in liquid form and bottled in gallon jugs; later he made tablets.

John Derringer was said to be a devout Christian and would not treat any man who swore or drank. He would treat no one he believed to be possessed by the devil.

John died in 1924 at the age of ninety-two. As time goes by and stories are told of John's life, they quickly add to the folklore of Kansas. There are many firsthand accounts of specific diagnoses and cures that people experienced in his lifetime. Modern research is proving the efficacy of some of the qualities of the plants and compounds that he prepared and used.

RANS BIKES: JERRELL NICHOLS

RANS bicycles were the brainchild of Randy Schlitter from Hays. Starting with sailing trikes and making his mark building recumbent

A Rans Dynamik. *Courtesy of RANS bikes, Montezuma.*

bicycles, those have become popular all around the world. Then, with the persuasion of a friend, he designed and built an ultra-light airplane. The RANS airplane business has gone worldwide, and the workforce has grown enough that the bicycle business was difficult to keep running at the same time.

Jerrell Nichols was a mechanic and bicycle enthusiast from the Mennonite community of Montezuma, which is southwest of Dodge City. Jerrell had experimented and built some bicycles on his own and one day drove up the road to Hays and visited with Randy about becoming a dealer. Randy and Jerrell became good friends, and eventually an agreement was made to sell the bicycle business and move manufacturing to Montezuma.

Jerrell and his wife grew up and are raising their family in Montezuma. Jerrell worked on farms in the area and was very mechanical, eventually starting his own automotive repair shop. Jerrell was also involved with the founding and operations of the Grey County Search and Rescue Team. When the wind farms were being built in Grey County, a review of safety procedures led the company to approach Jerrell and several members in the community with the idea of creating a rescue team. The team is independent of EMS and the fire department, but some of the members are also members of those organizations.

The members of the Rescue Team train once a month on high tower rescues and the procedures of working in grain elevators and wind towers. Members sometimes buy equipment and get training at their own expense. The team has invented rescue hardware that it builds and sells to other organizations. Once a year, the team goes to Colorado for training.

The town of Montezuma has a population of 1,000, so it is unusual for a manufacturer to be building bicycles in the middle of Western Kansas. Jerrell estimated that there are about 250 owners of the RANS bikes in town. He draws workers from the rural area and small towns of this region.

When the announcement was made that RANS bikes would be changing hands, it caused quite a ripple in the biking world. As the company grows and customers deal with Jerrell, his wife and the company, the brand and product seem to be in good hands. This is another example of small ideas becoming big ideas. This seems to be a common theme all through Kansas history.

ROSCOE CONKLING "FATTY" ARBUCKLE

Fatty Arbuckle was born in Smith Center on March 24, 1887, and weighed fourteen pounds. His father and mother were smaller-built people, and his father, William Arbuckle, swore that he could not have been the father and accused his wife of having an affair. In his indignation, Fatty's father named him after a politician he hated, Roscoe Conkling. His father was abusive and beat him regularly. The connection to Kansas was brief, but being born here makes him a Kansan and his story is a compelling one. History has not treated Fatty very kindly, and his story is one that most people never have heard—or if they did, they've heard versions that the crusaders of the time dictated.

The family moved to Santa Anna, California, in 1888. After Fatty's birth, his mother experienced constant health problems and abuse. One year after the family moved, she died. Fatty was abandoned by his father, and he survived by working in the kitchen of a hotel in San Jose. He sang to himself while working in the kitchen and soon caught the attention of another singer at the hotel. She encouraged him and soon got him into an amateur talent contest. While in the contest, he caught the eye of showman David Grauman, who soon had Fatty performing in vaudeville as a singer and dancer.

In 1904, Fatty joined the Pantages Theater Circuit and began touring the West Coast. While performing in San Francisco in 1906, he was caught in the San Francisco Earthquake and was forced to work clearing debris. Throughout his life, Fatty was a large man, most times weighing more than three hundred pounds. His name was not one that he chose, but it stuck for the rest of his life. His friends did not call him Fatty to his face. Even though a big man, he was a talented dancer and was extremely light on his feet and could do all kinds of dance steps and stunts.

In 1909, he appeared in his first movie, *Ben's Kid*, a Selig Production. He was very self-conscious and was so embarrassed about being in the film that he did not tell his friends about it. But that was not long to last. While touring with his new wife, Minata Durfee, through Hawaii, Japan and China, he was spreading his reputation as a talent. Working for Selig's Polyscope Company, he was soon moved to Keystone Studios, where he worked with Mabel Normand and Harold Lloyd.

While working as an actor, he was also a comedian, director and screenwriter and was soon mentoring Charlie Chaplin. He discovered Buster Keaton and was soon the most popular film star in Hollywood. He was the first one to make $1 million per year. He received advice from the opera star Enrico Caruso, who told him to "give up this nonsense you do for a living, with training you could be the second greatest singer in the world."

It was observed that Fatty could skip up the stairs as lightly as Fred Astaire. He could even do backward summersaults, which showed that he was a talented tumbler. But he put these talents into comedy. He was fond of the "pie in the face" gag, and the earliest known use of it by him was in the 1913 Keystone one-reeler *A Noise from the Deep*.

By 1916, his weight and heavy drinking were causing health problems. An infection in one leg developed into a serious carbuncle, and he almost lost the leg. During this time, he lost eighty pounds but became addicted to morphine. He started his own film company, called Comique, in partnership with Joseph Schenck. This company produced some of the best comedies of the era. At this time, Paramount offered Fatty a then unheard-of three-year contract paying $3 million. In order to take advantage of this offer, he transferred his ownership in Comique to Buster Keaton. He was to make eighteen pictures for Paramount under the terms of the deal.

Fatty was working very hard and decided to take a break. He had suffered second-degree burns on his buttocks from sitting on some acid accidentally on the set. With friends Lowell Sherman and Fred Fishback, the three checked into the St. Francis Hotel. Rooms 2019, 2020 and 2021 were occupied, using room 2020 as a party room. Several women were invited to the party one night, and Fatty was sleeping when he woke up to the noises.

According to the story and later testimony, Fatty was not happy about the party but soon got into the festivities nonetheless.

While the partying was going on, Fatty discovered actress Virginia Rappe incapacitated in the bathroom of one suite and summoned the hotel doctor and hotel manager. The doctor pronounced her as sick and drunk, and she was placed on a bed. Three days later, Rappe was admitted to the hospital, but there was no diagnosis as to what the problem was. She was getting sicker, and no one could detect any signs of trauma or bruising. Her friend Sydia Wirt was summoned by Rappe's manager to contact a party in New York about her illness. By the time the reply came, Rappe had died.

At autopsy, it was discovered that Rappe had a burst spleen. She was also known to have other health problems, one of them being that she was allergic to alcohol, and it was suspected that she had had a recent abortion. A woman who was at the party accused Fatty of having raped and beaten Rappe, causing her burst spleen. Although there was little evidence, the district attorney in San Francisco was ambitious and planning a run for governor, so he filed charges against Fatty.

Up to this time, studio owners in Hollywood were very strict about keeping a clean image of Hollywood and avoiding scandals. This was an opportunity for the newspapers and religious leaders who were against Hollywood to seize on this incident and make it into the first big scandal of Hollywood.

One of the people involved in the story, and for whom the truth didn't matter and no facts could be too bizarre, was William Randolph Hearst. His newspapers sensationalized the story and made millions. Even when the court trials came and no conviction was ever secured, it was definitely a case that was tried in the papers. The stories were exaggerated and sensationalized and ran nationwide. Although Fatty was a quiet and private man in his life away from the screen, he was portrayed as a gross lecher who used his weight to overpower women. Those who knew him said that he was very shy and good-natured. Hearst was ecstatic with the scandal and noted that "it sold more papers than any event since the sinking of the Lusitania."

The scandal ruined Fatty's career in Hollywood, and actors and producers were instructed to not use Fatty in any way or be associated with him. This was the first blacklisting in Hollywood. The trials became a sensation, although much of the testimony was refuted and the accuser was discovered to have extorted someone in her past and changed her story repeatedly.

Fatty was charged with manslaughter, although the DA wanted a first-degree murder charge filed. The first trial was declared a mistrial, as was a second trial. After a verdict of not guilty was delivered in the third trial, the jury stated that an apology should be given to Fatty for all the misery that he had gone through.

Regardless, Hollywood did not want Fatty to "work in this town again." The powers that be created a censor board, and the crusade against Fatty resulted in a majority of his work being destroyed. His wife divorced him, even though she proclaimed that Fatty was the "nicest man in the world." Fatty would later marry Doris Deane in 1925.

Later on, Fatty began to make a comeback, but alcoholism and a bad heart led to his death the day he signed a contract that would have officially brought him back. During his career, Fatty had discovered Buster Keaton and Bob Hope and encouraged Charlie Chaplin.

It was a long and harrowing journey for that baby from Smith Center to the height of the movies and then the depths of despair. He was torn down by those who had more to gain by attacking him than by searching for the truth. Fatty was a major innovator of slapstick comedy that made millions laugh. It is a tragedy that most of his work was destroyed.

WICHITA BLUE STREAK MOTORS

Wichita Blue Streak Motor Company is one of those companies that started with a leap into the sky-high expectations of the Wichita aviation scene. It is one of those stories that I found while researching others. Scanning the "Tihen Notes" of the Wichita State University Special Collections, the name jumped out at me.

The company was building an aircraft engine designed by Joseph Schaeffers. The patent was applied for on July 7, 1928, and was granted and published on October 7, 1930. The patent was assigned to the Blue Streak Motor Company in Wichita. Mentions in the *Wichita Eagle* newspaper put the location of the factory at 529 West Douglas. There is no mention of what aircraft the Blue Streak motors were put into. Production records indicate 70 engines were produced in 1929 of the 70-horsepower, two-cycle and dual-cylinder motor. Also, 125 motors were listed in 1929 for the 125-horsepower, five-cylinder radial engine.

Delano history notes that the factory built one- and two-seat airplanes that were used mostly for trainers. However, there are no records of the company actually building an airplane. There is a contract with Wichita University for the study of a motor for $200.

There is a note in an issue of *Aviation Week* for the election of J.A.F. Wright to replace Clyde M. Smyser. Smyser was one of the founders of the company. The company was short-lived; it is listed as running from 1929 to 1931.

In later years, Schaeffers was granted a patent on a similar design with assignment to himself.

With the lack of information, it is difficult to know what definitely happened to the company. However, the crash of 1929 also crashed the aircraft industry. In Wichita, there were only four companies that survived the crash and Depression.

WICHITA TRUNK FACTORY

Going back into old issues of the *Wichita Eagle* and *Wichita Beacon*, you will find advertisements for the Wichita Trunk Company. In today's world, with the fast pace and convenient luggage, the thought that trunks would be a good business may not make sense. But go back to the time when conditions of travel and just storing things to keep them clean, dry and free from rodents and pests would make trunks very important. Trunks were a very necessary item that almost everyone needed and possessed. Today, they are great collectibles, but you will find that many who have trunks for the aesthetics also utilize the trunk for storage.

The story of the Wichita Trunk Company is not an easy one to find. The ownership goes back to the Hossfeld family, especially Henry and George. George Hossfeld learned the trade in the trunk industry in Cincinnati, Ohio. Henry is listed as a trunk manufacturer in Kansas City in 1873, located at 1023 Market Street.

In April, George made a visit to Wichita, looking at the viability of locating a trunk factory and retail store. A month after coming to town, he started the business at 125 West Douglas. In 1928, the factory and store were listed at 233–235 South Main, opposite the city library. Advertisements were run in all the Wichita publications for the company.

An extensive story was run in the *Wichita City Eagle* on May 22, 1890, explaining the process by which the trunk body was made elsewhere, and all the hardware and assembly took place at the factory.

George's brother Henry ran a similar business in Topeka. That business was wiped out years later by a tornado and was not rebuilt. It is not quite clear if the Hossfelds' different trunk factories and retail stores were run as a family business unit or individually. In an obituary in the *Wichita Daily Eagle* on December 28, 1909, Henry is listed as being a Kansas City resident and secretary of the Hossfeld Trunk Manufacturing Company. He is listed as a former Wichitan. In the obituary, Henry also is listed as having brothers William, George, Charles and Edwin, as well as a sister, Mrs. Schaefer of Topeka, but it is certain that there were operations in Wichita, Topeka and Kansas City.

Looking at a list of trunk manufacturers in the United States shows that there were literally hundreds of companies, and all the surviving examples are now collectables.

RUDY LOVE

Rudy Love was born in Oklahoma, the oldest of fifteen children. The family moved to Wichita, and Rudy had to be the head of the family when his father, Robert, was on the road singing R&B and gospel music. His love of singing and the inspiration of his father prompted him to start his first band in grade school. Growing up, he was a member of several bands.

Additional inspiration came as he met the stream of artists who came through Wichita and were friends of his father's. When in college, Rudy formed the Rudy Love & the Love Family Band. Although very active, they did not record much in Wichita or at all. The discography only lists two singles: "Does Your Momma Know" and "Ain't Nothing Spooky," in 1975 and 1976, on Calla Records. Also one album, *This Song's for You*, for ATV/PYE Records.

At Calla Records, he wrote the best song on the Persuaders *All About Love* album, "Hey Sister I'm Your Brother." He issued two more singles on the Earthbound label: "Hungry Children" and "Then I Found You."

Rudy became a demo vocalist for Motown West and South, working under producers Clayton Ivy and Terry Woodford. He worked as band leader and manager for Sly Stone for ten years. He has written music for plays and performed in the Wichita area. His son, Rudy Love Jr., is an artist in the Los Angeles area.

Rudy assisted his mother, Ahnawake, in her popular soul food restaurant in Wichita, Mama Love's Kitchen, located on North Mosley in Old Town. The restaurant opened in 1998 and was known for its large, homemade portions and signature desserts. Mama Love died on September 15, 2011. Mama and Rudy are still remembered as a special part of Wichita.

The recorded works of Rudy Love & the Love Family Band are out of catalogue and are collectors' items today.

PHILLIP WEBB: HOISINGTON

Most heroes go about their lives not drawing attention to themselves, and Phillip Webb is one of those. In fact, finding information on Phil has been as hard as any subject. Not that he has faded into the historical past—Phil is very much alive as this is being written. Why would this quiet, humble man be a subject for this book? It is not the amount of time that has passed that makes one a part of Kansas history—it is the qualities of a person, as well as the acts that he has done, is still doing and will do that will be a part of history.

In fact, the only way I found out about Phil was because of that intrepid explorer of great stories Amy Bickle. In her *Hutchinson News* article of January 21, 2016, she told the story of Phil. In fact, it is about the only story in print I could find. But he was discovered also by Marci Penner and Wendee LaPlant in their search for information on their *Kansas Sampler Guide Book*. Also, the PBS show *Sunflower Journeys* did a story on Phil.

So, what is so special about Phil? Caring. Phil works a full-time job, and around the age of forty, he decided to explore his artistic side and took an art class. He started making concrete and steel sculptures for his and his wife's garden at home. He has sculptures of several famous people, including Neil Young and George Washington Carver.

As he found a passion making his sculpture, he also noticed many unmarked or barely marked graves in the Hoisington Cemetery. He became curious and started to look into the history of those buried and forgotten there. The monuments he started to make to mark graves were stumbled upon by Marcie and Wendee, and they were like nothing that they had seen before in the hundreds of cemeteries they had visited in their journeys around the state. Marci Penner is executive director for the Kansas Sampler Foundation. She commented that "the work that Phil has done here is a real treasure."

Asking about his work downtown, many never heard about his work. That does not bother him. The stories of the people he makes the monuments for are at the heart of *his* story—like the turret gunner of a B-17 in World War II who was shot down and spent the war in a Nazi *stalag*. Sergeant Neal Williams was liberated and awarded the Purple Heart, Bronze Star and Air Medal. He came home to live a quiet life, and when he died, he was shipped from his home in Warsaw, Missouri, to be buried at the Hoisington Cemetery. The mortuary had very little on him in its file, and there was no obituary. So, Phil researched his story and built a monument for him. Also noticing the unmarked grave of Creola Paxton, who had died in 1947, he asked an elderly man in town if he had known her, and he did.

There is a marker for an infant who died in 1955 and one for Lela Bailey, an African American woman who died one year following the death of her husband. When asked why, Phil just shrugs and says that it may be that some families were too poor to buy a stone. Whatever the reason, Phil tries to find the story and make a marker for the grave.

Phil does not look at himself as a great artist, but rather as someone who cares. Others believe that he is a great artist with a lot of heart and passion. As part of his concern, he contributes information and photos for the online site Find a Grave. By doing this, he helps families and others to find the grave site, see the marker and get a story about the person buried there.

WILLIAM FARMER: GOOFY

If you call Bill Farmer, born in Pratt, "Goofy," he will smile and say, "You are right!" And that is because he *is* Goofy. As a youth, he was fascinated with voices and would go through fast-food drive-ins and place orders like "I want a scotch and soda" as W.C. Fields. Fascinated by the Disney character Goofy, he would work on his voices and developed a great ability for executing them.

Going to the University of Kansas, he was soon involved with radio and TV work. He also started doing stand-up comedy in local clubs. He went

William Farmer of Pratt, Kansas, the voice of Goofy. *Courtesy of Wichita State University Library Special Collections.*

to Dallas, Texas, working at a comedy club called the Comedy Corner. A commercial agent suggested that he needed to move to California. Once there, his agent asked if he did any cartoon characters.

Bill's mentor was Daws Butler, the man behind many of the Hanna-Barbera cartoon character voices. His first audition was at Disney for the character of Goofy. He played Goofy in *A Goofy Movie* and *An Extremely Goofy Movie*. He was the voice of Goofy in the series of games *Goof Troop*.

Bill originated the voice of Horace Horsecallar. He also did additional voices on *The New Adventures of Mighty Mouse* and *Astro Boy*. He also played Yosemite Sam, Sylvester and Foghorn Leghorn in the movie *Space Jam*. He has done many other animated productions, including *Horton Hears a Who* and Daffy Duck in *Robot Chicken*.

In 2004, he started playing Doc, a character in the television series *The 7D*. He has more than one hundred celebrity impressions and dialects. He teaches, produces and does private coaching. His company is Toon House Inc.

GEECH: JERRY BITTLE

The creator of the comic strip *Geech* and later *Shirley and Son*, Jerry Bittle, was born in Heber Springs, Arkansas. When Jerry was two years old, his family moved to Wichita, and he went through school there, eventually attending Wichita State University. In his strips, the Geech character, based on him, was often seen wearing a WSU shirt.

He worked at the *Wichita Eagle* newspaper and started doing editorial cartoons for the paper. He then moved to the *Albuquerque Tribune*. Moving to Texas, he debuted the comic strip *Geech* in 1982. The strip's characters are based on many people in his life, as well as the businesses he grew up around. Starting out with the name *Crude*, a reference to oil field workers, the strip had a small-town appeal. He soon changed the name to *Geech* to capture a more universal appeal. His father was a barber and gave him a lot of background to base his humor on.

Jerry Bittle, cartoonist and creator of *Geech. Courtesy of Wichita State University Library Special Collections.*

Geech was started on a dare. Fans would tell him that they had grown up in that town. After a divorce, he debuted the strip *Shirley and Son. Geech* was syndicated in 175 newspapers, and *Shirley and Son* was syndicated in 75 papers.

Jerry died in Honduras of a heart attack on April 9, 2003, while on a family vacation.

PRISONERS OF WAR IN PEABODY

Driving through downtown in Peabody it may not be obvious, but during World War II, this was the location of a German prisoner of war internment facility. The two-story Eyestone Building was empty, and the War Department was looking for locations in the center part of the country to house POWs. The most well known of these was Camp Concordia; there are some remnants of the camp that can still be viewed today at the site just outside town.

The idea of bringing POWs to the Midwest was twofold. One was the ability to ensure that there was no reason to escape, as there was no way an escapee could ever make it back to Germany. Second was the fact that so many men were away fighting that there was a pressing need for labor on American farms. Another element was that if you keep someone busy, there was little opportunity to hatch plans or create problems.

Citizens were a little hesitant about having Germans living in camps near them. The few problems that started out with the camps were soon taken care of when army captain Karl Teufel was put in charge of organizing the education of prisoners. First, weeding out of the true Nazis removed the element that caused resistance to the occupation of the facilities. Also, the positive treatment and good food that was afforded the prisoners caught them totally by surprise. The treatment of Allied prisoners was not very good in the European Theater and was downright brutal and inhumane in the Pacific Theater. Some prisoners actually gained weight at the U.S. facilities.

The prisoners brought to the Eyestone Building in Peabody were housed on the main floor, and the guards were housed on the second floor. The building was constructed originally as a hotel during the oil boom of the 1920s. Nelson Poe acquired the building and mentioned to the Kansas Industrial Commission that he had a large, empty building that would be a good fit for a POW facility.

The prisoners brought to Peabody were all volunteers for farm work, and they had been screened carefully. Only prisoners who were screened by the U.S. Army Intelligence Division were approved and sent to Peabody. Most of the prisoners were in their thirties and forties, and several residents who spoke German volunteered to help communicate with them. Farmers' cars would line up in the mornings to take prisoner workers to their farms, especially during harvest time.

Even though the prisoners were supposed to eat the provisions supplied to them, many of the farm wives would feed the workers along with everyone else. Prisoners were allowed to bake German chocolate cakes and other pastries. Eventually, the prisoners were allowed to attend movies at the local movie theater on Sundays. The spectacle drew spectators from Wichita and Kansas City to see the prisoners dressed up in their uniforms marching to the movies. Residents were allowed to visit the prisoners, and many would bring pieces of wood that the POWs would carve into many things.

Many prisoners returned to Germany after the war, and some were so impressed with the United States that they immigrated back to the areas where they were held prisoner. Many became farmers, and their families are still here today.

BIRDMAN: ALBIN K. LONGREN

Albin Longren built one of the first motorcycles in Kansas. This was in 1904, one year before William Harley and Arthur Davidson road-tested their first motorcycle. And then Albin built an automobile while he was an automobile businessman in Clay Center. The editor of the *Leonardville Monitor* commented of the man who drove his automobile into town, "He made a car from practically nothing and it worked like a charm." Albin was twenty-three at the time.

In 1910, Albin attended a public demonstration in Topeka. A Curtiss Pusher plane flew in for the demonstration, but it crashed. Albin was fortunate enough to help with the repair of the aircraft. This inspired him to build an airplane of his own.

He did not want to bring attention to his project, and since he had no training in aircraft engineering, or even in flying such a craft, he worked quietly on his design. Renting the second floor of a building in Topeka, Albin, along with his brother, E.J. Longren, and a mechanic, William Janicke, worked on the design that Albin had been hashing out for his new airplane.

The men took the new airplane to a field outside town, not wanting to attract attention, and worked out any problems that it had. The first flight was about two feet high and two hundred feet long. Albin also needed the practice because he had never flown a plane before. He wanted to be competent before anyone saw him fly.

The airplane, named the *Topeka I*, was powered by a pusher propeller, similar to the Curtiss. In fact, there were several features that looked like they belonged on a Curtiss airplane. The plane also had a steering wheel and a three-wheel landing gear.

The airplane caused a lot of excitement at a Topeka exhibition. The local paper wrote about the flight, "He seemed in perfect control of his machine and the plane glided along through the air as smoothly as if it had been resting on the ground. There was not a ripple in the pathway, the craft cut through the sky, the turns were made in veteran style, and the second circle was completed before Longren dropped lightly to the ground."

Longren started an aircraft company and went on the barnstorming trail to bring attention to his aircraft and investors. This is when he earned the nickname of "Birdman." He flew the *Topeka V* on his barnstorming and crashed it. Upon repairing it, he sold the airplane to pilot Phil Billard, who had an earlier version of the airplane. Billard flew the airplane until he left for World War I. He was testing aircraft for the army when he crashed and

The *Topeka V*. Albin K. "Birdman" Longren was the first to manufacture airplanes in the state of Kansas. *Courtesy of the Kansas State Historical Society*.

was killed in Europe. The plane sat in the garage at the family home until 1938, when the family donated it to the Kansas State Historical Society, which has the *Topeka V* on display.

Albin's genius allowed him to not only build the first airplane in Kansas but also to improve on many other companies' airplanes with his patents. He played an important role in the U.S. government's first airplane development center. His first venture into building airplanes failed, however, and he had to declare bankruptcy. He had been flying into Leroy to meet with foreign investors, and he crashed and broke his leg, killing a cow in the process. The investors lost interest. Albin had built ten models of his airplane by this time, and quality was not his problem.

He met and married Dolly Trent, and she became a key partner in her husband's business. She would sew the wing covers and do other things around the factory. She came up with his business slogan "Watch it climb, see it fly, you'll own a Longren by and by."

Albin became the chief inspector of aircraft at McCook Field in Dayton, Ohio, during World War I. Here he mingled with all of the test pilots and designers and absorbed a massive amount of knowledge about aircraft and aircraft engineering. In 1919, he returned to Topeka to build an airplane that would be for "the doctor, the ranchman, the traveling man, and the farmer."

The model AK was called the "New Longren." It was nineteen feet long and weighed 550 pounds. The wings tucked, and the whole thing could be towed. There was a picture run in the *New York Times* of the plane at a filling station being fueled up. The new model plane was a two-seater, was equipped with a radial engine and could take off in a very short distance. The military was also impressed with the Longren airplane. The U.S. Navy aircraft lieutenant inspector of the Navy Bureau of Aeronautics was impressed with the airplane. Test pilot Lieutenant J.B. Kepp was so impressed with how the Longren airplanes handled that he recommended the navy purchase several of them. Kepp remarked that it "virtually landed itself." The navy was not convinced that the company had the resources to produce the number of planes that it wanted.

The other problem was that there were so many Curtiss Jennys available after World War I that the cost of the Longren was too high. Another problem was the fact that Longren was such a perfectionist that he would stop the assembly line to make a design change and was otherwise not easy to work for.

His marriage suffered, and amid the stress of a second business failure, the couple drifted apart. He spent a year in Canada vacationing. When he came back, he went to Tulsa, Oklahoma, and became vice-president of Mid-Continent Aircraft. The company would later become Spartan Aircraft. Because of his constant changes on the assembly line, he was eventually fired and went to San Antonio, Texas, where a group of businessmen asked him to design and build the "Alamo" airplane. The project disappeared along with about 80 percent of the aircraft industry in the 1929 Wall Street crash.

Albin did have a sense of history and legacy and assembled a collection of his work for the Kansas State Historical Museum. After this, he started working as a consultant rather than try to build another company. Even though he did not have a degree in aviation engineering, he was making a lot of improvements for others in the industry.

Albin had a contract with Butler Manufacturing and was involved in the production of the Butler Airplane. Only eleven Butlers were built before the company decided to concentrate on its agricultural product line.

Albin became good friends with Clyde Cessna and was hired to come to Cessna as vice-president. He brought his patents with him and made great contributions to the company. His biggest design was the hydraulic metal stretch process that allowed the outer skin to be fitted to the body of an airplane. This was when the transition from cloth to aluminum was taking place throughout the industry.

After leaving Cessna, Longren moved to California and had clients in Lockheed, Boeing and Northrup. Back in the former Blackhawk factory, Don Luscomb was building the Mono Coupe, which was the first mass-produced airplane with an all-aluminum skin—using Longren's patent.

The shame of it all is that Albin Longren had so much to do with the development of aircraft in the 1920s, 1930s and beyond but is virtually unknown in Kansas or outside aircraft circles. Not bad for a kid from Leonardville, however.

BIBLIOGRAPHY

40 & 8

Driskill, Silas. 40 & 8 member interview.

40 & 8 Lake, Garden Plain, Kansas.

History of 40 & 8. Brochure, n.d.

La Societe des Quarante Hommes et Huit Chevaux. http://www.fortyandeight.org.

Voiture Nationale, 40 & 8.

Charley Melvin: Iola's Mad Bomber

Get Rural Kansas. "Iola." https://www.getruralkansas.com.

Historical Newspapers from 1700s–2000s. www.newspapers.com.

Lynn, Susan. Interview with Judy Brownback, great-granddaughter. *Iola Register*. Daily Division 1, page 7. www.kspress.com/sites/default/files/transfer/2691922_newsandwriting.pdf.

Parsons Daily. "Is Melvin Bughouse?" September 14, 1905, 3.

Thrive, Allen County. "Charley Melvin Mad Bomber Run for Your Life." www.thriveallencounty.org.

Edgar Henry Summerfield Bailey

Bailey, E.H.S. Bailey Personal Papers, 1848–1973. University of Kansas, University Archives, Kenneth Spencer Research Library.

Berneking, Carolyn Bailey. "Pure Food and Water for Kansas: E.H.S. Bailey, the State Laboratory, and the State Board of Health during the Progressive Era." *Kansas History* 20, no. 1 (Spring 1997): 38–49.

Find a Grave. "Dr. Edgar Henry Summerfield Bailey." www.findagrave.com.

Hersey, Mark D. Department of History, University of Kansas.

McNaimer, Mike, Barber County Director of Public Health.

University of Kansas.

Beechcraft Plainsman Automobile

All Car Index. "United States Beechcraft Plainsman." https://www.allcarindex.com.

Blackwell, Nigel. "The Beechcraft Plainsman." www.nigelblackwell.com.

Curbside Classic. "Big Rear-Engined Four-Door Cars—Part 1: American Attempts." www.curbsideclassic.com.

How Stuff Works. www.howstuffworks.com.

Strohl, Daniel. *Hemmings Motor News.* September 9, 2007. https://www.hemmings.com.

Cloughley Motor Vehicle Company

Aldridge, Dorothy. "Early Traffic Situation in Colorado Springs Recalled." *Colorado Springs Gazette-Telegraph*, September 5, 1972, 13.

American Automobile. www.american-automobile.com.

Cherryvale Republican. "The Automobile Factory." September 5, 1901, 4.

Chetopa Clipper. "It Now Looks." May 22, 1902, 1.

Evening Herald (Parsons, KS). "The Parsons Automobile Factory." April 5, 1902, 5.

Evening Star (Independence, KS). "According to the Clarion." May 17, 1901, 1.

Find a Grave. "Robert H. Cloughley." https://www.findagrave.com.

Georgano, G.N. "Virtual Steam Car Museum." *Encyclopedia of American Automobile.* New York: E.P. Dutton & Company, 1968. www.virtualsteamcarmuseum.org.

Henry Ford Museum, 20900 Oakwood Boulevard, Dearborn, MI 48124. https://www.thehenryford.org.

Holton Signal. "The Cloughley Automobile." June 25, 1902, 7.

The Horseless Age 8, no. 2 (April 10, 1901): 204.

Mattox, David, and Mike Brotherton. *Images of America: Parsons.* Charleston, SC: Arcadia Publishing.

Modern Light (Columbus, KS). "Automobile Line for Columbus." November 21, 1905, 1.

The Motor Way. "1901 Automobiles." Vols. 4–5. N.p.: L.L. Bligh. GoogleBooks. https://books.google.com.

Parsons Daily Eclipse. "The Cloughley Automobile Is Noiseless." April 30, 1902, 4.

Parsons Daily Sun. March 11, 1916, 4. Kansas Historical Open Content. https://kansashistoricalopencontent.newspapers.com.

Parsons Library. http://parsons.mykansaslibrary.org.

Goddard's Bush Pilot

Alaska Bush Pilot. "Roy Dickson." http://alaskabushpilot.org.

Anchorage Daily News. "Alaska Aviation Legends: For Warren Thompson, Safety, Service Came First." October 10, 2014. https://www.adn.com.

Levi, Steve. *Cowboys of the Sky: The Story of Alaska's Bush Pilots.* 2nd ed. N.p.: Publication Consultants, 2008.

Pierce, Dennise. *Wichita Eagle.* N.d.

Rearden, Jim, and James Anderson. *Arctic Bush Pilot: From Navy Combat to Flying Alaska's Northern Wilderness.* N.p.: Epicenter Press, 2000.

Staheli, Lee. *At the Last Frozen Minute.* N.p.: Xlibris Corporation, 2009.

Kansas Volcano

Evening Kansan Republican (Newton, KS). "Cracks in Earth Causing Worry." August 23, 1911, 5.

Historical Newspapers from 1700s–2000s. www.newspapers.com.

Kansas Geological Survey. Harper County.

Parker, J.D. *Earthquake in Kansas.* Kansas State Historical Sec. Trans, v. 12. N.p., 1912, 121–31.

Sanders, Gwendoline, and Paul Sanders. *The Harper County Story.* 1st ed. Newton, KS: Mennonite Press, 1968.

White, Edward, and Ethel Loany. Genealogy Trails, August 24, 1900. http://genealogytrails.com.

Wichita Searchlight. "Earth Splits in Kansas." August 23, 1911.

Marion and Maude Frakes: Maude's Rock Garden

Coffeeville Daily Journal. "Drowned in Elk River." March 28, 1912, 8.

Elk County: A Narrative History of Elk County and Its People. Elk County Historical Society, 1986, 63.

Evening Star (Independence, KS). "Marion Frakes." February 14, 1913, 5.

Find a Grave. "Maude B. Frakes, Elk Falls Cemetery." www.findagrave.com.

Frakes, Elizabeth M., daughter-in-law.

Frakes family scrapbook.

Fry, Steve. Elk Falls Pottery.

Independent (KS) Daily Reporter. "Marion Frakes of Elk Falls." October 8, 1912, 6.

Iola Register. "Mr. Marion Frakes." August 24, 1934, 3.

———. "Mrs. May Puckett Returned." April 30, 1947, 3.

Tanner, Beccy. *Hutchinson News.* July 25, 2016, A5.

———. "Secret Elk County Garden Is Uncovered." *Hutchinson News*, July 24, 2016.

Unruh, Cheryl. "The Hidden Garden." *Emporia Gazette*, June 7, 2011. www.emporiagazette.com.

Massey Harris Company: Hutchinson Factory

Historical Newspapers from 1700s–2000s. www.newspapers.com.

Hutchinson News. "History of Massey Harris Harvestor in Hutchinson, Kansas, 1924–1940." Articles of that period, Reno County Historical Museum.

———. "Massey-Harris Company a Very Large Concern." May 21, 1925, 5.

Massey Harris: A Historical Sketch, 1846–1926. Toronto: Massey-Harris Press, 1926.

Moore, Sam. "The Merger of Massey and Harris." *Farm Collector*, November 2008.

Reno County Historical Society Museum.

Ottawa Manufacturing Company

Ottawa Manufacturing Company, Franklin County, Kansas. Kansas Memory, Kansas State Historical Society. Dated between 1950 and 1970. www.kansasmemory.org.

Ottawa Mule Team ad. www.ottawamuleteam.com.

Wells, Brian Wayne. "Ottawa Manufacturing Company of Ottawa Kansas." *Belt Pulley Magazine* 11, no. 3 (May–June 1998).

Sidney Toler: Charlie Chan

Find a Grave. "Sidney Toler." www.findagrave.com.

Kansapedia. "Sidney Toler/Charlie Chan." Kansas Historical Society. https://www.kshs.org/kansapedia/kansapedia/19539.

Wichita Beacon. "Sidney Toler, Wichitan." February 13, 1921, 3, 21–22.

Skunk Johnson

Cutler, William G., ed. *History of the State of Kansas*. Chicago: A.T. Andreas, 1883. https://onlinebooks.library.upenn.edu.

Kansapedia. "Skunk Johnson." Kansas Historical Society.

Pratt Kansas Heritage Group. www.kansastowns.us.

Wichita City Eagle. "'Skunk' Johnson Returns to Cave after 38 Years." February 12, 1911, 3.

The Green Top

Author and family memories.

Johnson, June. Neighborhood newsletter, August 24, 2014.

Practical Builder. "An Eye-Catcher on the Highway." August 1962, 67.

Tragic Happening on the Ninnescah

Coffee shop legend.

Dorthy Renner Kraus Diary. Handwritten account.

Patricia Renner and family member interviews.

Twin Windmill Company

American Wind Power Museum, Lubbock, Texas. https://windmill.com.

Baker, T. Lindsay. "Blowin' in the Wind." Kansas State Historical Society. https://www.kshs.org/publicat/history/1996spring_baker.pdf.

Bickel, Amy. *Hutchinson News*. July 19, 2011, A1 and A5.

Kansas Companies. https://www.kansasregistry.com.

Reno County Historical Museum.

Westbrook, Ray. "Twin-Wheel Windmill Restored to Its Former Glory." *Lubbock Avalanche-Journal*, February 8, 2012. www.Lubbockonline.com.

U.S. Guyer

Archer, Jules. *The Plot to Seize the White House*. New York: Skyhorse Publishing, 2007.

Biographical Directory of the Congress of the United States, 1774–Present. "Ulysses Samuel Guyer, 1868–1943." Washington, D.C.: United States Congress.

Find a Grave. "Ulysses Samuel Guyer #6635725." www.findagrave.com.

Guyer family archives.

Hathaway, Michael, Curator. "U.S. Guyer." Stafford County Museum, Stafford, Kansas. http://museum.staffordcounty.org.

Viola Springs Water: Charles G. Davis

Access Genealogy. "Biography of Charles Wood Davis." https://accessgenealogy.com.

American Bottler 37 (n.d.): 49.

Connelley, William Elsey. *A Standard History of Kansas and Kansans*. Vol. 3. N.p.: Facsimile Publisher, 2015. Reprint.

Cutler, William G., ed. *History of the State of Kansas*. Part II, *Sedgwick County*. Township Sketches. Chicago: A.T. Andreas, 1883.

Department of the Interior, U.S. Geological Survey. *Mineral Resources of the U.S., 1918*. Part II, *Nonmetals*. Washington, D.C.: Government Printing Office, 1921.

Genealogy Trails. "Kansas Trails. Sedgwick County, Viola." http://genealogytrails.com.

Historical Newspapers from 1700s–2000s. www.newspapers.com.

Sedgwick County Register of Deeds.

A Twentieth Century History and Biographical Record of Crawford County, Kansas. Madison: University of Wisconsin, The Printery, 1976. Digitized on September 11, 2012.

Wichita Beacon. "At the Exposition." October 17, 1913, 10.

———. "Is Bottled Only Right at Springs." July 20, 1920, 5.

———. "State Board of Health Reports." June 25, 1922, 19.

———. "Viola Informs Wichita It Has Pure Soft Water to Spare." July 21, 1913, 2.

———. "A Water Famine Is Threatening." July 28, 1913, 2.

———. "Would Pipe Soft Water to City from Ninnescah." January. 28, 1923, 3.

Wichita City Directories.

Wichita City Library, Research Department.

Wichita Daily Eagle. "Asks to Be Fish Warden." February 9, 1915, 1.

———. "Call 125 Witnesses." May 4, 1915, 2.

———. "Hit by a Motor Truck." December 21, 1921, 6.

———. "Puts Six Questions." May 6, 1915, 5.

———. "Sheriff's Sale." October 6, 1881.

———. "Typhoid Has Commenced." June 29, 1918, 10.

———. "Viola Springs Water." June 24, 1918, 9, advertisement.

———. "Whole County Is Interested in Ice Plant." May 1, 1917.

Volco Manufacturing Company

Anthony Bulletin. Clip. November 9, 1922, 1.

Anthony City Library.

Anthony Republican. "Volco Refinery for Anthony." March 18, 1926.

Bragg, G.A. "Investigation of Soap Powders." ETD_1913_Bragg_GA_Medium.pdf. https://kuscholarworks.ku.edu, 13.

Historical Newspapers from 1700s–2000s. www.newspapers.com.

Kansas Geological Survey, Harper County.

Kansas Historical Society.

Lumber Mfg. & Dealer 69.

Topeka Capital Journal. "Volco Manufacturing Co. Makes Topeka Sales Headquarters." February 8, 1914, 21.

Volco Manufacturing Company, Kansas Secretary of State Office.

Wichita Beacon. "Asks Receiver be Appointed for Volvo Co." November 4, 1922, 5.

———. "Have You Been Closely Following…." June 8, 1912, 8.

———. "Suing the Volco Company for Audit and Other Work." March 11, 1922, 10.

———. Volco advertisement. October 3, 1912, 12.

———. "The Volco Company's Stockholders…." January 6, 1921, 6.

Wichita City Eagle. "Volco Manufacturing Company is Being Backed Strongly by Prominent Wichitans." December 26, 1920, 31.

Wichita Daily Eagle. "Boost for Volco." December 20, 1921, 3.

———. "Creditors to Meet." November 19, 1922, 4.

———. "Find Deposit of Rare Clay." August 31, 1922, 7.

———. "Harper." October 9, 1914, 10.

———. "Industrial Side." February 16, 1920, 5.

———. "Make Dirt Fly with 'Volco.'" March 27, 1919, 1.

———. "May Borrow $5,000." December 13, 1922, 5.

———. "Soap Made by the Volco Company is of Particularly High Quality." December 26, 1920, 31.

———. "Valuable Deposits Volcanic Ash Found Near Anthony, KS." February 16, 1910, 8.

———. "Volcanic Ash among Assets." November 21, 1922, 11.

———. Volco advertisement. March 16, 1919, 2.

———. "Volco Assets Are Fixed at $515,000." December 8, 1922, 3.

———. "Volco Campaign Starts." January 5, 1914, 4.

———. "Volco Cleaner Is Wichita Product." March 9, 1921, 9.

———. "Volco Makes a Clean Home." March 30, 1919, 3.

———. "Wanted Sales Ladies." March 7, 1921, 6.

Wichita Eagle. "Tihen Notes." September 23, 1923. Wichita State University Special Collections.

Wichita Public Library.

W.A. Dye Chili, Wichita

Dye Chile Company. C.A. Seward, Prairie Print Makers.

Flickr. www.flickr.com.

Historical Newspapers from 1700s–2000s. www.newspapers.com.

National Register of Historic Places, United States Department of the Interior.

Wichita Daily Eagle. "American 'Pep' Made in Wichita Helped Win War."
   March 16, 1919, 2.
———. Classified display advertisements. December 16, 1920, 1.
———. Classified display advertisements. February 20, 1916, 1.
———. "Mr. W.A. Dye." March 16, 1919, 2.

Walker Family Inventions

Vintage Puller. www.vintagepullers.com.
Walker Mowers. "The Walker Story." www.walker.com.

Wichita Tractor

Joplin Museum Complex, Joplin, Missouri City Directory.
Kansas Secretary of State. Agrimotor Manufacturing Company Charter.
———. Change of name resolution. National Tractor Company Charter.
Kansas State Historical Society.
Old Iron, Iron Age Memories 6.
Steel Processing & Conversation 7, no. 7. Information on forging and heat
   treating.
Wendel, C.H. *Standard Catalog of Farm Tractors, 1890–1980.* 2nd ed. N.p.,
   1980, 701.
Wichita Beacon. "Tihen Notes." Wichita State University Special Collections.

Wichita: Broom Corn Capital

The Broom Factory: The Atlantic-Southwestern Broom Company. Harbor
   Enterprises Center LLC. http://www.broomfactory.com.
Wichita Beacon. "Tihen Notes." Wichita State University Special Collections.
   Southwestern Broom & Warehouse, 1908.
Wichita Daily Eagle. "The Little Lady Broom." March 16, 1919, 2.
———. "Wichita Is Largest Broom Corn Market in World." September 24,
   1922, 50.
———. "Wichita Is the Largest Broom Corn Market in the World." October
   3, 1920, 25.
———. "World's Greatest Broom Corn Sold in Wichita." May 12, 1912, 34.

Supreme Propellers

Flying Magazine 17, no. 3 (September 1935): 172.

Price, J.M. *Wichita's Legacy of Flight.* Charleston, SC: Arcadia Publishing, 2003.

Wichita Beacon and *Wichita Eagle.* "Tihen Notes." Wichita State University Special Collections. specialcollections.wichita.edu/collections/local_history/tihen/pdf/beacon/Beac1928.pdf, specialcollections.wichita.edu/collections/local_history/tihen/pdf/eagle/Eag1929.pdf.

Wings Over Kansas—Vintage Aircraft. https://wingsoverkansas.com.

Pelican Pete: Elias Pelton

Find a Grave. "Elias Pelton." www.findagrave.com.

Hanks, Kathy. "A Marsh Fellow Tale: 'Pelican Pete' Made It His Home; Eccentricities Recalled." *Hutchinson News,* January 6, 2016. www.hutchnews.com.

O'Hara, Betty, great-niece.

Stafford County Historical Museum. "Pelican Pete, Paul Bunyan of the Salt Marsh." http://staffordcounty.org. Reprinted from the *Ellinwood Leader,* May 17, 1945.

Krause Torque Tractor

Antique Power Magazine.

Krause Kuhn. "Tillage Tools." https://www.kuhn-usa.com.

McDaniel, Leslie. "Two of a Kind." Farm Collector "Before & After," April 2001. https://www.farmcollector.com.

Garlic Salad

Harris, Anita. "Garlic Salad." Food.com.

Neil, Denise. "Doc's Steak House Will Close in October After 62 Years in Business." "Dining with Denise," *Wichita Eagle,* September 18, 2014.

Postings by Veronica. "Aunt Ruby's Copycat Garlic Salad." https://reciperhapsody.file.wordpress.com.

Harold Ensley: The Sportsman's Friend

Ensley, Harold. Kansas Sports Hall of Fame, inducted in 2005.

Find a Grave. "Harold Ensley." www.findagrave.com.

Frazee, Brent. "Harold Ensley; Show on Fishing Ran for 48 Years." Knight Ridder, August 26, 2005.

Arkalon and the Mighty Samson

Chinn, Jack. "Causes and Clean Up of Train Wreck." *Pratt Tribune,* June 16, 1993.

———. "The 'Samson of the Cimarron.'" "Along the Museum Trail," *Pratt Tribune Extras*, November 6, 1991, 6.

———. "This Bit of Railroad History." *Pratt Tribune*, May 5, 1993, 8.

Geographic Names Information System (GNIS). Arkalon, Kansas. United States Geological Survey (USGS), October 13, 1978. http://geonames.usgs.gov.

Kansas Sampler Foundation. "Mighty Samson of the Cimarron, Seward County." 8 Wonders of Kansas. www.kansassampler.org.

Moree, Keeley. "Mighty Samson Bridge Nears 73rd Birthday." *Leader Times Newspaper*, May 5, 2012.

The Rocket. "The Samson Bridge Set a World Record." December 1944.

Bert Wetta Sales

Hall, Tyler D. *Performance/Endurance: The Men and Machines of Field Queen Incorporated*. N.p.: self-published, 2015.

U.S. Alfalfa Company. "History." www.usalfalfa.net.

U.S. Alfalfa Company. www.usalfalfa.net.

U.S. Greens. "History." usgreens.net.

Field Queen

Major information was provided by Tyler D. Hall, who spent four years researching the company and wrote the definitive history of Field Queen, *Performance/Endurance: The Machines and Men of Field Queen* (self-published, 2015).

U.S. Alfalfa Company. www.usalfalfa.net.
U.S. Greens. "History." usgreens.net.

Dorothy Delay

Ancestry.com. Dorothy Delay in the 1940 census.
Barber County Index. "Birth Announcement." April 9, 1919, 10.
————. "Medicine Lodge Orchestra." December 21, 1910, 1.
————. "Widely Known Couple Married." February 16, 1916, 1.
Emporia Gazette. "Glenn A. Delay Heads Curriculum Department."
    September 5, 1945, 1.
————. "Grove-DeLay." August 10, 1936, 6.
Facebook. Marsha Hoagland page.
Find a Grave. "Dorothy Delay Newhouse." www.findagrave.com.
Historical Newspapers from 1700s–2000s. www.newspapers.com.
Horvath, Janet. "The Great Women Artists Who Shaped Music II: Dorothy
    DeLay." *Interlude,* April 25, 2015.
Kansapedia. "Dorothy DeLay." Kansas Historical Society.
Pittsburgh Post-Gazette. "Dorothy Delay, Julliard Instructor Acclaimed as
    World's No. 1 Violin Teacher." March 26, 2002. Obituaries. old.post-
    gazette/obituaries/20020326delayobit0326page2.asp.
————. "Obituary: Dorothy Delay, Julliard Instructor Acclaimed as World's
    No. 1 Violin Teacher." March 26, 2002. www.post-gazette.com.
Sand, Barbara Lourie. *Teaching Genius: Dorothy Delay and the Making of a
    Musician.* Washington, D.C.: Amadeus Press, 2000.

Fort Scott Foundry and Machine Company: Albert W. Walburn

Annual Report of Railroad Commissioners, issue no. 4, 1886.
Fort Scott Daily Monitor. "The History of the Walburn-Swenson Company."
    April 13, 1893, 5.
————. "Local Development." March 24, 1889, 1.
Fort Scott Weekly Monitor. "Electric Light Co." January 2, 1890, 23.
Harper's Magazine 85. Advertiser (n.d.): 26.
Historical Newspapers from 1700s–2000s. www.newspapers.com.
Indian Journal (Muskogee, OK). Fort Scott Foundry, advertisement. April 1,
    1880.

Kansas State Historical Society.

Leavenworth Weekly Times. "The Machinery of Walburn Swenson." December 29, 1892, 7.

Parsons Eclipse. Fort Scott Foundry, advertisement. February 1, 1878.

Sedalia Democrat. "Obituary." October 15, 1930, 9.

Sedalia Weekly Bazoo. "Cupid's Couples." December 4, 1883, 6.

Sedalia Weekly Democrat. "Mrs. Albert Walburn." September 27, 1940.

Smithsonian Libraries. Trade catalogues from Fort Scott Foundry and Machine Works Company.

Sugar Cane 25 (February 1, 1893).

Topeka Capital Journal. Fort Scott Foundry and Machine Work, advertisement. October 18, 1881.

Frankfort: Ultimate Sacrifice

Brunner, Melissa. *News Leader*. "Frankfort Boys Highway to Be Dedicated." *Kansas News Leader*, June 15, 2012. https://www.wibw.com.

Fry, Steve. "'Frankfort Boys' on Road to Immortality." *Topeka Capital Journal*, January 21, 2012. https://www.cjonline.com.

Kessinger, Sarah. "Town Suffered Highest Casualty Count for Town Its Size." *Marysville Advocate*, June 20, 2012. www.marysvilleonline.net.

Gilbert Twigg: Mass Murderer

Historical Newspapers from 1700s–2000s. www.newspapers.com.

Krajicek, David J. "Mass Shooter 'Crazy Twigg,' Who Killed Nine at 1903 Kansas Concert, Sent Message to Future Gunmen." *New York Daily News*, June 18, 2016. http://www.nydailynews.com.

Weinman, Sarah. "How a Forgotten 1903 Killing Spree Became America's First Modern Mass Shooting." Buzzfeed, March 24, 2016. https://www.buzzfeed.com.

Wellington Daily News. "Insane Man." August 14, 1903, 1. Kansas Historical Open Content. https://kansashistoricalopencontent.newspapers.com.

Winfield Courier. "The Camen Band Massacre—Mass Murder in Winfield in 1903." August 14, 1903.

Gunny

Clark, Doug. "Gunny Has a Terrifying Bark, but Won't Bite." *Spokesman-Review*, April 24, 2011. R. Lee Ermey personal website. http://www.rleeermey.com.

Cooper, Steve. "Gunny R. Lee Ermey Unplugged." *The First Shot*, September 2010. http://odcmp.org.

R. Lee Ermey personal website. http://www.rleeermey.com.

Ira D. Brougher: Barton County

Barton County, Kansas Archives. "Ira Brougher Biography." http://files.usgwarchives.net.

Bickel, Amy. "Unions Soldier Statue Repaired; Celebration Planned." *Hutchinson News*, November 1, 2015. www.hutchnews.com.

Biographical History of Barton County, Kansas. Great Bend, KS: Tribune Publishing Company, 1912. Digitized on February 23, 2008, and available online at http://www.archive.org/details/biographicalhist00grea.

Brougher, Ira. *Great Bend Tribune.* October 22, 1886, 4. Historical Newspapers from 1700s–2000s. https://img5.newspapers.com.

Find a Grave. "Ira D. Brougher." www.findagrave.com.

Kansas Civil War Memorials and Monuments. "Barton County, Kansas." http://www.kscwmonuments.com.

Jesse Harper: Kansas Rancher Who Hired Knute Rockne

Clark County Historical Society newsletter, December 2013. Pioneer-Krier Museum. www.pioneer-krier.com/Newsletter2013-Dec.pdf.

Clark County Historical Society newsletter, November 2016. Pioneer-Krier Museum. www.pioneer-krier.com/Newsletter2016-Nov.pdf.

National Football Foundation. "Jesse Harper." https://footballfoundation.org.

Notre Dame Athletics. "Jesse Harper: The Game Changer." August 29, 2013. https://und.com.

Pumlee, Rick. "Kansas Ties to Notre Dame Go Beyond Rockne Crash Scene." *Wichita Eagle*, September 26, 1999. https://www.chicagotribune.com.

Shank, Richard. "A Kansas Ranchers Legacy in Notre Dame Football." *Hutchinson News*, December 27, 2018. www.hutchnews.com.

B-29 Tragedy at Copeland

American Safety Network. "Accident Boeing B 29 Super Fortress 42-6379." September 17, 1944. https://aviation-safety.net.

Anzanos, Andrew. *Stories of a B-17 Pilot*. N.p.: Lulu.com, 2013.

Beitler, Stu. "Copeland, KS Bomber Crashes into Home." *Hutchinson News Herald*. September 19, 1944. https://www.gendisasters.com.

Cimarron Jacksonian. September 21, 1944.

390th Bomb Group: 50th Anniversary Commemorative History. N.p.: Turner Publishing, 1994.

Ward, E. Faye. *History of Early Day Copeland, Kansas, 1912–1965*. E. Faye Ward family, 1977. https://books.google.com.

Bailor Plow Manufacturing Company

Atchison Daily Globe. "Local Factory Possibilities." April 14, 1921, 2. https://newspapersarchive.com.

———. "Will Discuss Bailor Affairs." April 13, 1921, 2. https://newspaperarchive.com.

Atchison Historic Resources Survey. September 25, 1998. https://www.kshs.org/resource/survey/AtchisonHistoricResourcesSurvey1998.pdf. Kansas State Historical Society.

Implement and Tractor 32, no. 2 (1917): 20.

Moore, Patty. "The Man Who Cultivated Atchison." Atchison Globe Now, June 28, 2010. http://www.atchisonglobenow.com.

Moore, Sam. "Let's Talk Rusty Iron: An Idea Whose Time Never Came." *Farm Collector Magazine* (June 2005). https://www.farmcollector.com.

Roby, Barbara, and Rick Mannen. "The Indiana Mule." *Antique Power Magazine* (n.d.): 68–70.

Wendel, C.H. *Standard Catalog of Farm Tractors, 1890–1980*. N.p.: Bailor Plow Manufacturing Company.

Baughman Farms

Find a Grave. "Captain Henry Clay Baughman." www.findagrave.com.

———. "John William Baughman." www.findagrave.com.

Genuine Kansas. "Famous Kansans: Philip Anschutz, Businessman." http://www.genuinekansas.com.

Hutchinson News. "Baca County Colorado Wheat Land." September 12, 1929, 6.

Kansapedia. "John W. Baughman." Kansas Historical Society. https://www.kshs.org.

Liberal Democrat. "All Eyes Are Turned Toward the West." June 3, 1920.

———. "The Cause of Production." May 30, 1918.

———. "Missed the Train." June 3, 1920.

———. "You Know What Sherman Said About War." May 30, 1918.

Blue Valley Manufacturing and Foundry

Baker, Lindsey T. *A Field Guide for Windmills*. 1st ed. Norman: University of Oklahoma Press, 1985.

Find a Grave. "Abby Lillian Marlatt #36691233." www.findagrave.com.

———. "Fredrick Albert Marlatt #117195158." www.findagrave.com.

Marlatt, Fredrick A. "Kansas Trails." Kansas State Historical Society.

Riley County Historical Society Museum. Linda Glascow, Curator of Archives and Library.

Wendel, C.H. *Encyclopedia of American Farm Equipment and Antiques*. Iola, WI: Krause Publications, 1977.

Lone Tree Massacre, 1874

Kansas Memory, Kansas State Historical Society. Correspondence on the Lone Tree Massacre. https://www.kansasmemory.org.

Lookingbill, Brad D. *War Dance at Fort Marion: Plains Indian War Prisoners*. Norman: University of Oklahoma Press, 2006.

Mendoza, Patrick M., Ann Strange Owl–Raben and Nico Strange Owl. *Four Great Rivers to Cross: Cheyenne History, Culture, and Traditions*. N.p.: Libraries Unlimited, 1998.

Montgomery, Mrs. F.C. "United States Surveyors Massacred by Indians (Lone Tree, Meade County, 1874)." *Kansas Historical Quarterly* 1, no. 3 (May 1932): 266–72. https://www.kancoll.org.

New York Times. "Surrender of an Indian Tribe." February 27, 1875.

Ohnick, Nancy. "Tragedy on Crooked Creek." *Hometown Magazine* (Spring 1993). Copyright Ohnick Enterprises. Old Meade County. http://www.oldmeadecounty.com.

What Kansas's Shape Could Have Been

Collections of the Kansas State Historical Society. "The Boundary Lines of Kansas." www.kshs.org.

Martin, George W. "The Boundary Lines of Kansas." Presented before the Old Settlers Association. Published by Nabu Public Domain Reprints.

Kansas Wildlife Law Enforcement

Hesket, Dan. Kansas Department of Wildlife, Parks and Tourism.

Mead, J.R. *Hunting and Trading on the Great Plains, 1859–1875.* 1st ed. Norman: University of Oklahoma Press, 1986.

Quail, Leland. Interviews.

Alta Mill

Kansas Ghost Towns. "Dead Towns of Kansas." December 16, 2011. www.kansasghosttowns.blogspot.com.

Peters, Grant. "Alta Mills, Harvey County." Lost Communities. https://lostkscommunities.omeka.net.

Stucky, Brian D., ed. The Alta Milling Company, Moundridge, Kansas. www.altamill.org.

Stucky, Renae. "Growth and Decline of the Alta Mills Community: A Case Study of Dead and Dying Towns in Kansas." Swiss Mennonite Cultural and Historical Association, April 7, 2016. www.swissmennonite.org/wp-content/uploads/2018/11/rise_fall-alta.pdf.

Swiss Mennonite Cultural and Historical Association. "Alta Mill Story." www.swissmennonite.org/wp-content/uploads/2019/04/Alta-Mill-Story.pdf.

Anthony Benton Gude

Anthony Benton Gude. https://anthonybentongude.com.

The Artist's Road. "Anthony Benton Gude." https://www.theartistsroad.net.

Biles, Jan. "Benton Gude: An Artist's Legacy." *Topeka Capital Journal*, March 2, 2008.

Gude, Anthony Benton. Strecker-Nelson Gallery. https://snwgallery.com.

Kansas City Times. "Obtains a Divorce." March 11, 1965, 3.

Kiechel Fine Art. "Anthony Benton Gude." https://kiechelart.com.

Norman, Bud. "Artist Follows Famous Footsteps." *Wichita Eagle*, December 29, 2002, 1E, 2E.

Auto-Fedan Hay Press Company

Emporia Gazette. Advertisement. May 28, 1910, 5.

Junction City Daily Union. "At Work at the Hay Camp." July 16, 1913, 1.

Manning, Dan R. "Hay Rake and Hay Press Make One Rare Pair." *Farm Collector*, August 2014. https://www.farmcollector.com.

Ross, Edward P. "Kansas Trails." Kansas State Historical Society.

Wendel, C.H. *Encyclopedia of American Farm Equipment and Antiques.* Iola, WI: Krause Publications, 1977.

Who's Who in the Kansas City Manufacturers Exposition. Auto-Fedan Hay Press Company, November 1912. http://www.vintagekansascity.com.

Yesterday's Tractors. Auto-Fedan Hay Press.

Buckskin Joe

Arkansas City Daily Traveler. "Buckskin Joe Is Dead." April 22, 1918, 2.

Arkansas City Traveler. "Buckskin Joe." June 27, 1905, 2.

Civil War Talk Forum. "Buckskin Joe." https://civilwartalk.com.

Colorado Virtual Library. "Horace Tabor: The Silver King." www.coloradovirtuallibrary.org.

Grout, Pam. *Kansas Curiosities.* 3rd ed. Guilford, CT: Globe Pequot Press, 2010, 120.

Historical Newspapers from 1700s–2000s. www.newspapers.com.

Emanuel Haldeman-Julius: Hero/Antihero

Appeal to Reason. Historical Newspapers from 1700s–2000s. https://www.newspapers.com.

Girard, Kansas. https://www.girardkansas.gov.

Haldeman-Julius: Pocket Series and the Little Blue Books. www.haldeman-julius.org.

Kansapedia. "Haldeman-Julius, Marcet, and Emanuel Haldeman-Julius." Kansas Historical Society. https://www.kshs.org.

Kansas Memory, Kansas State Historical Society. Emanuel Haldeman-Julius. https://www.kansasmemory.org.

Draining the McPherson Wetlands

Ducks Unlimited. "McPherson Wetlands Get Use." https://www.ducks.org.

———. "Restoring the McPherson Wetlands Project." https://www.ducks.org.

Kansas Department of Wildlife, Parks and Tourism.

The Ledger. August 20, 2001.

McPherson Daily Republican. "Toad Plague." June 29, 1901, 1. Historical Newspapers from 1700s–2000s. https://www.newspapers.com.

Queal, Leland. Interviews and historic materials.

OMC Tractor: Ostenberg Motor Parts Company

Aberdeen News. "OMC Was Kansas Tractor." December 12, 2008. http://articles.aberdeennews.com.

Antique Power Magazine (July/August 2006). https://www.antiquepower.com.

Beattie, David. McPherson, Kansas.

Farm Collector Magazine. "The Golden Roll" (September/October 1995). http://www.farmcollector.com.

Gas Engine Magazine (December 1990).

———. "OMC Tractor" (January/February 1993). http://www.gasenginemagazine.com.

———. "Rare Canadian Norseman" (August/September 1993).

Hoffman, Ray. "OMC Tractors." *Antique Power Magazine* (March/April 1991): 20–24.

Norseman tractor Smokstak, online discussion site. https://www.smokstak.com.

Parsons, Irvin. OMC collector.

Salina Journal. "Antique Engine Show." August 13, 1993, 28.

———. F. Amos Ostenberg obituary. February 15, 1980, 11.

———. "Lute Ostenberg Dead at 64." Obituary, March 6, 1964, 2.

Wendel, C.H. *Standard Catalog of Farm Tractors, 1890–1980.* 2nd ed. N.p., 1980, 604.

Yesterday's Tractors. "OMC Tractors/Rare." https://www.yesterdaystractors.com.

Sinkhole Sam

Adrian, Jack, and Vicki Adrian. Interview.

Capps, Chris. "The Strange Tale of Sinkhole Sam." June 15, 2010. Unexplainable. www.unexplainable.net.

Dewey. Ernest. "Monster Turns Out to Be a Plain Old Foopengerkle." *Salina Journal,* November 23, 1952, 12.

Flynn, Mary K. *Leavenworth Times.* October 15, 1953. Historical Newspapers from 1700s–2000s. www.newspapers.com.

———. "Sighted Sink-Hole Sam, but Couldn't Sink Same." *Abilene Reporter-News,* December 28, 1953, 5.

Gilliland, Steve. "The Legend of Sinkhole Sam." *The Kansan* (Newton, KS). June 12, 2010. https://www.thekansan.com.

Morphy, Rob. "The Legend of Sinkhole Sam." Cryptopia. https://www.cryptopia.us/site/2010/06/the-legend-of-sink-hole-sam.

Notoriously Morbid. "Sinkhole Sam." March 10, 2018. https://notoriouslymorbid.com.

Penner, Marci. Interview.

Cash Hollister: Caldwell Lawman

Baker, Kim. "Obituary for Cassius 'Cash' Hollister, B. 1845 OH, D. 1884 KS." Genealogy. https://www.genealogy.com. From *Caldwell Journal,* October 23, 1884, 3.

Caldwell Journal. "A Man for Supper, Killed Because He Would Not Surrender." November 23, 1883.

Find a Grave. "Cassius M 'Cash' Hollister." www.findagrave.com.

Hollister, Cassius M. (Cash). Roots Web ID118404. www.ancestry.com.

National Law Enforcement Officers Memorial.

Neal, Bill. *Encyclopedia of Western Gunfighters*. Norman: University of Oklahoma Press, 1991.

Rizzo, Tom. *Tall Tales from the High Plains and Beyond*. N.p.: Amazon Digital Services LLC, 2015.

George Grant: Mr. Angus

American Angus Association. "Kansas Profile: Victoria, Kansas, The Cradle of US Angus." August 20, 2009. http://www.angus.org.

The Borrowed Book. "Did You Know? Sir George Grant and the Colony of Victoria." March 2014. http://theborrowedbook.blogspot.com.

Breeds of Livestock–Angus Cattle. Oklahoma State University. http://afs.okstate.edu.

Explore Rural Kansas; Get Rural Kansas. "George Grant Villa." www.getruralkansas.org.

Forsyth, James L. "George Grant of Victoria: Man and Myth." *Kansas History* 9, no. 3 (n.d.): 102–14. Kansas State Historical Society. https://www.kshs.org/publicat/history/1985autum_forsythe.pdf.

Raish, Marjorie Gamet. *Victoria: The Story of a Western Kansas Town*. N.p.: F. Voiland Jr., state printer, 1947.

Saddle Butte Ranch. "In the Beginning." http://www.saddlebutteranch.com.

Jacob John "Indian John" Derringer

Biles, Jan. *Topeka Capital Journal*. July 18, 2004. http://old.cjonline.com.

Find a Grave. "Jacob John 'Indian John' Derringer, Memorial #76891166." www.findagrave.com.

Historical Newspapers from 1700s–2000s. www.newspapers.com.

Kansapedia. Kansas Historical Society.

Tanner, Beccy. "Herbal Cures Just Part of Legend." *Salina Journal*, March 8, 1981, 56.

RANS Bikes: Jerrell Nichols

Backcountry Pilot. "RANS Sells Bicycle Division; More Emphasis on Planes?" https://backcountrypilot.org.

Kansas Sampler Foundation.

Krieg, Martin. "National Bicycle Greenway." Podcast transcript, July, 13, 2015. http://www.ransbikes.com.

KSFFA's Fire News Blog. "Gray County Search and Rescue Team." June 23, 2016. https://ksffa.blog/2016/06/23/gray-county-search-and-rescue-team-unique-to-sw-kansas-area.

Loewen, Rudy. "Gray County Rescue Team Unique to SW Kansas Area." *Montezuma Press*, June 2, 2016.

RANS Bikes. http://www.ransbike.com.

Recumbent and Tandem Rider. "RANS Changing Hands." January 28, 2015.

Roscoe Conkling "Fatty" Arbuckle

Find a Grave. "Roscoe Fatty Arbuckle." www.findagrave.com.

International Buster Keaton Society. http://www.busterkeaton.org. Website owned and run by Melisa Tallmadge Cox, granddaughter.

King, Gilbert. "The Skinny on the Fatty Arbuckle Trial." Smithsonian Institution, November 8, 2011. www.smithsonian.com.

Rosenberg, Jennifer. "The 'Fatty' Arbuckle Scandal." Updated May 9, 2018. https://www.thoughtco.com.

Sheerin, Jude. "Fatty Arbuckle and Hollywood's First Scandal." BBC News, September 4, 2011.

Wichita Blue Streak Motors

Aerofiles. Aviation Week, 29. www.aerofiles.com.

Blue Streak Motors. https://www.geocaching.com.

Historic Delano. www.historicdelano.com.

Wichita Beacon. "Tihen Notes." 1928. Wichita State University Special Collections. http://specialcollections.wichita.edu/collections/local_history/tihen/pdf/beacon/Beac1928.pdf.

————. "Tihen Notes." 1929. Wichita State University Special Collections. http://specialcollections.wichita.edu/collections/local_history/tihen/pdf/beacon/Beac1929.pdf.

————. "Tihen Notes." 1927. Wichita State University Special Collections. http://specialcollections.wichita.edu/collections/local_history/tihen/pdf/beacon/Beac1927.pdf.

———. "Tihen Notes." Wichita State University Special Collections. http://specialcollections.wichita.edu/collections/local_history/tihen/pdf/beacon/Travel_Air.pdf.

Wichita Eagle. "Tihen Notes." 1931. Wichita State University Special Collections. http://specialcollections.wichita.edu/collections/local_history/tihen/pdf/eagle/Eag1931.pdf.

Wings Over Kansas: State, National and International Aviation, Aeronautics & Aerospace Resources. https://wingsoverkansas.com.

Wichita Trunk Factory

Antique Trunk Makers—Brettuns Village. https://www.brettunsvillage.com.

Hills, Bentley O. *History of Wichita and Sedgwick County, Kansas: Past and Present.* Vol. 1. Chicago: C.F. Cooper & Company, 1910. https://www.amazon.com.

Kansas State Labor Department. 23rd Report, 1907.

Wichita Beacon. "Tihen Notes." Wichita State University Special Collections. http://specialcollections.wichita.edu/collections/local_history/tihen/pdf/beacon/Beac1928.pdf.

Wichita Daily Eagle. Obituary, Henry Hossfeld. December 28, 1909.

———. "Wichita Trunk Company." January 25, 1911, 6.

———. "Wichita Trunk Factory." May 22, 1890, 5.

Rudy Love

Guest, J.C. "Rudy Love, Exposing the Legend." *Splurge Magazine.* http://www.splurgemag.com.

Hamilton, Andrew. "Rudy Love." AllMusic. https://www.allmusic.com.

KMUW—Wichita Public Radio. "Wichita's Rudy Love & The Love Family 'Funkumentary' Comes to Tallgrass." https://www.kmuw.org.

Maue, Savanna. "Film about Kansas Singer and Songwriter Rudy Love Wins International Accolades." December 22, 2018. https://www.cjonline.com.

Riedel, Matt. "Wichita Musician to Know—Rudy Love, Jr." *Wichita Eagle,* October 6, 2016. https://www.kansas.com.

Phillip Webb: Hoisington

Bickle, Amy. "Concrete Devotion: Resident's Graveside Folk Art Accents Unique Aspects of Departed Lives." *Hutchinson News*, January 21, 2016. www.hutchnews.com.

Sunflower Journeys. PBS, episode no. 2811. https://www.pbs.org.

William Farmer: Goofy

Bill Farmer personal website. www.billfarmer.net.

D23 Walt Disney Archives. "Bill Farmer." http://d23.com.

Voice Chasers. "Bill Farmer." http://www.voicechasers.com.

Geech: Jerry Bittle

Find a Grave. "Jerry Wanye Bittle, Allen, Collin County, Texas." www.findagrave.com.

Lambiek Comiclopidia. "Jerry Bittle." https://www.lambiek.net.

Los Angeles Times. "Jerry Bittle, 53; Created Comic Strip 'Shirley and Son'." April 11, 2003. https://www.latimes.com.

The Shocker. "In Memorium, Jerry Bittle, Creator of 'Geech'" (Spring 2003). http://wsu.wichita.edu.

Tanner, Beccy. "Creator of 'Geech' Comic Strip Grew Up in Wichita." *Wichita Eagle*, July 30, 2012. https://www.kansas.com.

Weekly Storybook. "Sunday Profile: Jerry Bittle on 'Shirley and Son'." March 20, 2010. https://www.weeklystorybook.com.

Prisoners of War in Peabody

Epps, Melvin D. "German POWs in Peabody Kansas: 1943–1946." Frederic Remington Area Historical Society. http://remingtonhistoricalsocietyks.org.

May, Lowell A., and Mark P. Schock. *Prisoners of War in Kansas—1943–1946*. Manhattan, KS: KS Publishing Inc., 2007. https://www.amazon.com.

Middleton, Patricia. "Veteran Remembers POW Camp in Peabody." *The Kansan*, July 7, 2016. https://www.thekansan.com.

O'Brien, Patrick G., Thomas D. Isern and R. Daniel Lumley. *Stalag Sunflower: German Prisoners of War*. Topeka: Kansas State Historical Society, 1984.

Plett, Rowena. "POW-Carved Gift Taxies into Permanent Home." *Peabody Gazette-Bulletin*. Last modified February 7, 2019. www.peabodykansas. com.

Birdman: Albin K. Longren

Kansapedia. "Longren's Biplane." Kansas Historical Society. https://www. kshs.org.

Kansas Memory, Kansas State Historical Society. Longren Airplane Company. https://www.kshs.org.

Lambertson. Giles. "The Birdman of Topeka." *Air & Space Magazine* (July 22, 2015). https://www.airspacemag.com.

Tanner, Beccy. "Hat, Scarf Belonging to Kansas' First Aviator." *Wichita Eagle*, August 4, 2017. https://www.kansas.com.

INDEX

ABOUT THE AUTHOR

Roger Ringer is a lifelong country boy growing up working on his grandfather and uncle's farm. Joining the volunteer organization Civil Preparedness Heavy Rescue Unit in Sedgwick County, the experience led him to join the Sedgwick County Fire Department. Still working on farms and ranches, he retired from the fire service and ran his own private detective agency for several years. He attended several colleges and universities, accumulating hours in fire, rescue and emergency medical technician training, re-certification and assisted in training exercises. Roger was certified as an Emergency Medical Technician—Ambulance in 1976 and retired his certification in 2010.

He went to Worldwide College of Auctioneering in Mason City, Iowa, and was in the auction business for several years. Working in family businesses, he still spent many hours on horseback and on the seat of a tractor. He is inflicted with "Old Iron Fever" and has bought and sold many antique and classic tractors over the years. He has owned and operated a portable hay mill and ground hay for ranches, farms and dairies over a three-county area.

Roger operated road graders for two townships and was a township trustee for one term. He has welded, carpentered and wood-carved.

After the loss of a friend, he returned to writing poetry and began to perform cowboy and country poetry in the region around south-central Kansas. He then turned to western music and regularly attended the Western Music Association Festival in Albuquerque, New Mexico. He has been onstage at the Cowboy Symposium in Lubbock, Texas, and performed on stages in Dodge City, Wichita, St. Joseph, Missouri and many other cities and towns. He was a founding member and vice-president for the Kansas chapter of the Western Music Association, retiring recently. He is a life member of the Western Music Association and a board member of the Cowboy Storytellers Association of the Western Plains and publishes the organization's newsletter.

Always a history buff, he spent two years at Old Cowtown Museum in Wichita, Kansas, where he played the part of Fritz Schnitzler, a local saloon and business owner in early Wichita. Interpreting for visitors required more than a thumbnail amount of knowledge. During the off season, he works in maintenance and helps build and rebuild exhibits.

Roger has been a writer for years and does a weekly blog column that is published in several papers. He has published a book of country and cowboy poetry and one CD of western music. He is known for his love of history and rural Kansas. Roger has lived his whole life in rural Kansas and has no plans to change that. He owns a nearly seven-hundred-volume research library on western history and Kansas history.

Roger published his first book, called *Kansas Oddities: Just Bill the Acting Rooster, the Locust Plagues of Grasshopper Falls, Naturalist Camps and More*, on little-known Kansas history. He still lives in the Gypsum Hills of south-central Kansas and continues to research and find stories of Kansas that have been forgotten and need to be saved.

Visit us at
www.historypress.com